Russell & Russell 11-61 (Sweringen)

HISTORICAL MATERIALISM

HISTORICAL MATERIALISM

AND

THE ECONOMICS OF
KARL MARX

BENEDETTO CROCE

Translated by C. M. Meredith
and with an introduction by A. D. Lindsay

NEW YORK
RUSSELL & RUSSELL · INC
1966

FIRST PUBLISHED IN 1914
BY GEORGE ALLEN & UNWIN LTD.

REISSUED, 1966, BY
RUSSELL & RUSSELL, DIVISION OF ATHENEUM HOUSE, INC.
BY ARRANGEMENT WITH FRANK CASS & CO. LTD., LONDON
L.C. CATALOG CARD NO: 66-15950

Printed in Great Britain

21862

CONTENTS

CHAPTER III

CONCERNING THE INTERPRETATION AND CRITICISM OF SOME CONCEPTS OF MARXISM

CHAPTER IV

RECENT INTERPRETATIONS OF THE MARXIAN
THEORY OF VALUE AND CONTROVERSIES CON-
CERNING THEM

I

II

Meaning of phrase crisis in Marxianism : Sorel's
view of equivalence of value and labour mostly
in agreement with view put forward above :
An attempt to examine profits independently

CHAPTER V

A CRITICISM OF THE MARXIAN LAW OF THE FALL IN THE RATE OF PROFITS

CHAPTER VI

ON THE ECONOMIC PRINCIPLE

TWO LETTERS TO PROFESSOR V. PARETO

I

II

INTRODUCTION

THE Essays in this volume, as will be apparent, have all of them had an occasional origin. They bear evident traces of particular controversy and contain much criticism of authors who are hardly, if at all, known in this country. Their author thought it worth while to collect them in one volume and it has been, I am sure, worth while to have them translated into English, because though written on different occasions and in different controversies they have all the same purpose. They are an attempt to make clear by philosophical criticism the real purpose and value of Marx's work.

It is often said that it is the business of philosophy to examine and criticise the assumptions of the sciences and philosophy claims that in this work it is not an unnecessary meddler stepping in where it is not wanted. For time and again for want of philosophical criticism the sciences have overstepped their bounds and produced confusion and contradiction. The distinction between the proper spheres of science and history and moral judgment is not the work of either science or history or moral judgment but can only be accomplished by philosophical reflection, and the philosopher will justify his work, if he can show the various contending parties that his distinctions will disentangle the puzzles into which they have fallen and help them to understand one another.

The present state of the controversy about the value of the writings of Karl Marx obviously calls for some such work of disentangling. No honest student can deny that his work has been of great historic importance and it is hard to believe that a book like *Das Kapital* which has been the inspiration of a great movement can be nothing but a tissue of false reasoning as some of its critics have affirmed. The doctrine of the economic interpretation of history has revivified and influenced almost all modern historical research. In a great part of his analysis of the nature and natural development of a capitalist society Marx has shown himself a prophet of extraordinary insight. The more debatable doctrine of the class war has at least shown the sterility of the earlier political theory which thought only in terms of the individual and his state. The wonderful vitality of the Marxian theory of labour value in spite of all the apparent refutations it has suffered at the hands of orthodox political economists is an insoluble puzzle if it had no more in it than the obvious fallacy which these refutations expose. Only a great book could become ' the Bible of the working classes.'

But the process of becoming a Bible is a fatal process. No one can read much current Marxian literature or discuss politics or economics with those who style themselves orthodox Marxians without coming to the conclusion that the spirit of ecclesiastical dogmatism daily growing weaker in its own home has been transplanted into the religion of revolutionary socialism. Many of those whose eyes have been opened to the truth as expounded by Marx seem to have been thereby granted that faith which is the faculty of believing what we should otherwise know to be untrue, and with them the economic interpretation of history is transformed into a metaphysical dogma of deterministic materialism. The philosopher naturally finds a stumbling-block in a doctrine which is proclaimed but not argued. The historian however grateful he may be for the light which economic interpretation has given him, is up in arms against a theory which denies the individuality and uniqueness of history and reduces it to an automatic repetition of abstract formulæ. The politician when he is told of the universal nature of the class war points triumphantly to the fact that it is a war which those who should be the chief combatants are slow to recognise or we should not find the working classes more ready to vote for a Liberal or a Conservative than for a Socialist. The Socialist must on consideration become impatient with a doctrine that by its fatalistic determinism makes all effort unnecessary. If Socialism must come inevitably by the automatic working out of economic law, why all this striving to bring it about? The answer that political efforts can make no difference, but may bring about the revolution sooner, is too transparently inadequate a solution of the difficulty to deceive anyone for long. Lastly the economist can hardly tolerate a theory of value that seems to ignore entirely the law of supply and demand, and concludes with some justice that either the theory of labour value is nonsense or that Marx was talking about something quite apart in its nature from the value which economics discusses. All these objections are continually being made to Marxianism, and are met by no adequate answer. And just as the sceptical lecturer of the street corner argues that a religion which can make men believe in the story of Balaam's ass must be as nonsensical as that story, so with as little justice the academic critic or the anti-socialist politician concludes that Socialism or at least Marxianism is a tissue of nonsensical statements if these ridiculous dogmas are its fruit.

A disentangler of true and false in so-called Marxianism is obviously needed, and Senatore Croce is eminently fitted for the work. Much of the difficulty of Marx comes from his relation to Hegel. He was greatly influenced by and yet had reacted from Hegel's philosophy without making clear to others or possibly to himself what his final position in regard to Hegel really was. Senatore Croce is a Hegelian, but a critical one. His chief criticism of Hegel is that his philosophy tends to obscure the individuality and uniqueness of history, and Croce seeks to avoid that obscurity by distinguishing clearly the methods of history, of science and of philosophy. He holds that all science deals with abstractions, with what he has elsewhere called pseudo-concepts. These abstractions have no real existence, and it is fatal to confuse the system of abstraction which science builds up with the concrete living reality. 'All scientific laws are abstract laws,' as he says in one of these essays, (III p. 57), 'and there is no bridge over which to pass from the concrete to the abstract ; just because the abstract is not a reality but a form of thought, one of our, so to speak, abbreviated ways of thinking. And although a knowledge of the laws may *light up* our perception of reality, it cannot become that perception itself.'

The application to the doctrine of historic materialism is obvious. It calls attention to one of the factors of the historical process, the economic. This factor it quite rightly treats in abstraction and isolation. A knowledge of the laws of economic forces so obtained may 'light up our perception' of the real historical process, but only darkness and confusion can result from mistaking the abstraction for reality and from the production of those *a priori* histories of the stages of civilisation or the development of the family which have discredited Marxianism in the eyes of historians. In the first essay and the third part of the third Croce explains this distinction between economic science and history and their proper relation to one another. The second essay reinforces the distinction by criticism of another attempt to construct a science which shall take the place of history. A science in the strict sense history is not and never can be.

Once this is clearly understood it is possible to appreciate the services rendered to history by Marx. For Croce holds that economics is a real science. The economic factors in history can be isolated and treated by themselves. Without such isolated treatment they cannot be understood, and if they are not understood, our view of history is bound to be unnecessarily narrow and onesided. *On the relative importance* of the economic and the political and the religious factors in history he has nothing to say. There is no *a priori* answer to the question whether any school of writers has unduly diminished or exaggerated the importance of any one of these factors. Their importance has varied at different times, and can at any time only be estimated empirically. It remains a service of great value to have distinguished a factor of such importance which had been previously neglected.

If then the economic factor in history should be isolated and treated separately, how is it to be distinguished? For it is essential to Croce's view of science that each science has its own concepts

which can be distinguished clearly from those
of other sciences. This question is discussed in
Essay III Q. 5 and more specifically in Essay VI.
Croce is specially anxious to distinguish between
the spheres of economics and ethics. Much confusion has been caused in political economy in
the past by the assumption that economics takes
for granted that men behave egoistically, *i.e.* in an
immoral way. As a result of this assumption men
have had to choose between the condemnation of
economics or of mankind. The believer in humanity
has been full of denunciation of that monstrosity
the economic man, while the thorough-going
believer in economics has assumed that the success
of the economic interpretation of history proves
that men are always selfish. The only alternative
view seemed to be the rather cynical compromise
that though men were sometimes unselfish, their
actions were so prevailingly selfish that for political
purposes the unselfish actions might be ignored.
Croce insists, and surely with justice, that economic
actions are not moral or immoral, but in so far
as they are economic, nonmoral. The moral
worth of actions cannot be determined by their
success or failure in giving men satisfaction. For
there are some things in which men find satisfaction which they yet judge to be bad. We must
distinguish therefore the moral question whether
such and such an action is good or bad from the
economic whether it is or is not useful, whether
it is a way by which men get what they, rightly or

wrongly want. In economics then we are merely discussing the efficiency or utility of actions. We can
ask of any action whether it ought or ought not
to be done at all. That is a moral question. We
may also ask whether it is done competently or
efficiently: that is an economic question. It might
be contended that it is immoral to keep a public
house, but it would also have to be allowed that
the discussion of the most efficient way by keeping
a public house was outside the scope of the moral
enquiry. Mrs Weir of Hermiston was confusing
economics with ethics when she answered Lord
Braxfield's complaints of his ill-cooked dinner by
saying that the cook was a very pious woman.
Economic action according to Croce is the condition of moral action. If action has no economic
value, it is merely aimless, but it may have economic
value without being moral, and the consideration
of economic value must therefore be independent
of ethics.

Marx, Croce holds was an economist and not
a moralist, and the moral judgments of socialists
are not and cannot be derived from any scientific
examination of economic processes.

So much for criticisms of Marx or rather of
exaggerated developments of Marxianism, which
though just and important, are comparatively
obvious. The most interesting part of Signor
Croce's criticism is his interpretation of the shib-
boleth of orthodox Marxians and the stumbling-
block of economists, the Marxian theory of labour

value with its corollary of surplus value. Marx's exposition of the doctrine in *Das Kapital* is the extreme of abstract reasoning. Yet it is found in a book full of concrete descriptions of the evils of the factory system and of moral denunciation and satire. If Marx's theory be taken as an account of what determines the actual value of concrete things it is obviously untrue. The very use of the term surplus value is sufficient to show that it might be and sometimes is taken to be the value which commodities ought to have, but none can read Marx's arguments and think that he was concerned with a value which should but did not exist. He is clearly engaged on a scientific not a Utopian question.

Croce attempts to find a solution by pointing out that the society which Marx is describing is not this or that actual society, but an ideal, in the sense of a hypothetical society, capitalist society as such. Marx has much to say of the development of capitalism in England, but he is not primarily concerned to give an industrial history of England or of any other existing society. He is a scientist and deals with abstractions or types and considers England only in so far as in it the characteristics of the abstract capitalist society are manifested. The capitalism which he is analysing does not exist because no society is completely capitalist. Further it is to be noticed that in his analysis of value Marx is dealing with objects only in so far as they are commodities produced by labour. This is evident enough in his argument. The basis of his contention that all value is 'congealed labour time' is that all things which have economic value have in common only the fact that labour has been expended on them, and yet afterwards he admits that there are things in which no labour has been expended which yet have economic value. He seems to regard this as an incidental unimportant fact. Yet obviously it is a contradiction which vitiates his whole argument. If all things which have economic value have not had labour expended on them, we must look elsewhere for their common characteristic. We should probably say that they all have in common the fact that they are desired and that there is not an unlimited supply of them. The pure economist finds the key to this analysis of value in the consideration of the laws of supply and demand, which alone affect all things that have economic value, and finds little difficulty in refuting Marx's theory, on the basis which his investigation assumes.

A consideration of Marx's own argument forces us therefore to the conclusion that either Marx was an incapable bungler or that he thought the fact that some things have economic value and are yet not the product of labour irrelevant to his argument because he was talking of economic value in two senses, firstly in the sense of price, and secondly in a peculiar sense of his own. This indeed is borne out by his distinction of value and price. Croce developing this hint, suggests that

the importance of Marx's theory lies in a comparison between a capitalist society and another
abstract economic society in which there are no
commodities on which labour is not expended, and
no monopoly. We thus have two abstract societies,
the capitalist society which though abstract is very
largely actualised in modern civilisation, and another
quite imaginary economic society of unfettered
competition, which is continually assumed by the
classical economist, but which, as Marx said, could
only exist where there was no private property in
capital, *i.e.* in the collectivist state.

Now in a society of that kind in which there
was no monopoly and capital was at everyone's
disposal equally, the value of commodities would
represent the value of the labour put into them,
and that value might be represented in units of
socially necessary labour time. It would still have
to be admitted that an hour of one man's labour
might be of much greater value to the community
than two hours of another man, but that Marx
has already allowed for. The unit of socially
necessary labour time is an abstraction, and the
hour of one man might contain two or any number
of such abstract units of labour time. What Marx
has done is to take the individualist economist at his
word : he has accepted the notion of an economic
society as a number of competing individuals. Only
he has insisted that they shall start fair and therefore that they shall have nothing to buy or sell
but their labour. The discrepancy between the

values which would exist in such a society and actual prices represent the disturbance created by the fact that actual society is not a society of equal competitors, but one in which certain competitors start with some kind of advantage or monopoly.

If this is really the kernel of Marx's doctrine, it bears a close relation to a simpler and more familiar contention, that in a society where free economic competition holds sway, each man gets what he deserves, for his income represents the sum that society is prepared to pay for his services, the social value of his work. In this form the hours worked are supposed to be uniform, and the differences in value are taken to represent different amounts of social service. In Marx's argument the social necessity is taken as uniform, and the difference in value taken to represent differences in hours of work. While the main abstract contention remains the same, most of those who argue that in a system of unfettered economic competition most men get what they deserve, rather readily ignore the existence of monopoly, and assume that this argument justifies the existing distribution of wealth. The chief purpose of Marx's argument is to emphasise the difference between such an economic system and a capitalist society. He is here, as so often, turning the logic of the classical economists against themselves, and arguing that the conditions under which a purely economic distribution of wealth could take place, could only exist in a community where monopoly had been completely abolished and all capital collectivised.

Croce maintains that Marx's theory of value is economic and not moral. Yet it is hard to read Marx and certainly Marxians without finding in them the implication that the values produced in such an economic society would be just. If that implication be examined, we come on an important difficulty still remaining in this theory. The contention that in a system of unfettered economic competition, men get the reward they deserve, assumes that it is just that if one man has a greater power of serving society than another he should be more highly rewarded for his work. This the individualist argument with which we compared Marx's assumes without question. But the Marxian theory of value is frequently interpreted to imply that amount of work is the only claim to reward. For differences in value it is held are created by differences in the amount of labour. But the word amount may here be used in two senses. When men say that the amount of work a man does *should* determine a man's reward ; they commonly mean that if one man works two hours and another one, the first ought to get twice the reward of the second. 'Amount' here means the actual time spent in labour. But in Marx's theory of value amount means something quite different, for an hour of one man's work may, he admits, be equal to two of another man's. He means by amount a sum of abstract labour time units. Marx's scientific theory of value is quite consistent with different abilities getting different rewards, the moral contention that men should get more reward if they work more and for no other reason is not. The equation of work done by men of different abilities by expressing them in abstract labour time units is essential to Marx's theory but fatal to the moral claim sometimes founded upon it.

Further the great difficulty in allowing that it is just that men of different abilities should have different rewards, comes from the fact that differences of ability are of the nature of monopolies. In a pure economic society high rewards would be given to rare ability and although it is possible to equate work of rare ability with work of ordinary ability by expressing both as amounts of abstract labour time units, it surely remains true that the value is determined not by the amount of abstract labour time congealed in it but by the law of supply and demand. Where there are differences of ability there is some kind of monopoly, and where there is monopoly, you cannot eliminate the influence of the relation of supply and demand in the determination of value. What you imagine you have eliminated by the elimination of capital, which you can collectivise, remains obstinately in individual differences of ability which cannot be collectivised.

But here I have entered beyond the limits of Croce's argument. His critical appraisement of Marx's work must be left to others to judge who

have more knowlege of Marx and of economics
than I can lay claim to. I am confident only that
all students of Marx whether they be disciples or
critics, will find in these essays illumination in a
field where much bitter controversy has resulted
in little but confusion and obscurity.

A. D. LINDSAY.

CHAPTER I. CONCERNING THE SCIENTIFIC FORM OF HISTORICAL MATERIALISM

HISTORICAL materialism is what is called a fashionable subject. The theory came into being fifty years ago, and for a time remained obscure and limited ; but during the last six or seven years it has rapidly attained great fame and an extensive literature, which is daily increasing, has grown up around it. It is not my intention to write once again the account, already given many times, of the origin of this doctrine ; nor to restate and criticise the now well-known passages in which Marx and Engels asserted the theory, nor the different views of its opponents, its supporters, its exponents, and its correctors and corruptors. My object is merely to submit to my colleagues some few remarks concerning the doctrine, taking it in the form in which it appears in a recent book by Professor Antonio Labriola, of the University of Rome [1].

For many reasons, it does not come within my province to praise Labriola's book. But I cannot

[1] *Del materialismo storico, dilucidazione preliminare*, Rome, E. Loescher, 1896. See the earlier work by the same author : *In memoria del 'Manifesto dei communisti,'* 2nd ed. Rome, E. Loescher, 1895.

help saying as a needful explanation, that it appears to me to be the fullest and most adequate treatment of the question. The book is free from pedantry and learned tattle, whilst it shows in every line signs of the author's complete knowledge of all that has been written on the subject: a book, in short, which saves the annoyance of controversy with erroneous and exaggerated opinions, which in it appear as superseded. It has a grand opportunity in Italy, where the materialistic theory of history is known almost solely in the spurious form bestowed on it by an ingenious professor of economics, who even pretends to be its inventor [1].

I

1. *Scope of essay: Labriola's book implies that historical materialism is not a philosophy of history: Distinction between a philosophy of history and philosophising about history: Reason why two have been confused: Materialistic theory of history as stated by Labriola not an attempt to establish a law of history: This contrasted with theories of monists, and teleologists: Engels' statement that it is a new method erroneous: New content not new method.*

ANY reader of Labriola's book who tries to obtain from it a precise concept of the new theory of history, will reach in the first instance a conclusion which must appear to him evident and incontestable, and which I sum up in the follow-

[1] I refer to the works of Professor Achille Loria.

ing statement : ' historical materialism, so-called, *is not a philosophy of history.*' Labriola does not state this denial explicitly ; it may even be granted that, in words, he sometimes says exactly the opposite.[1] But, if I am not mistaken, the denial is contained implicitly in the restrictions which he places on the meaning of the theory.

The philosophical reaction of realism overthrew the systems built up by teleology and metaphysical dogmatism, which had limited the field of the historian. The old philosophy of history was destroyed. And, as if in contempt and depreciation, the phrase, ' to construct a philosophy of history,' came to be used with the meaning : ' to construct a fanciful and artificial and perhaps prejudiced history.'

It is true that of late books have begun to reappear actually having as their title the ' philosophy of history.' This might seem to be a revival, but it is not. In fact their subject is a very different one. These recent productions do not aim at supplying a *new philosophy of history*, they simply offer *some philosophising about history*. The distinction deserves to be explained.

The possibility of a philosophy of history presupposes the possibility of reducing the sequence of history to general concepts. Now, whilst it is possible to reduce to general concepts the particular factors of reality which appear in history

[1] He calls it on one occasion : ' the final and definite philosophy of history.'

and hence to construct a philosophy of morality or of law, of science or of art, and a general philosophy, it is not possible to work up into general concepts the single complex whole formed by these factors, *i.e.* the *concrete fact*, in which the historical sequence consists. To divide it into its factors is to destroy it, to annihilate it. In its complex totality, historical change is incapable of reduction except to one concept, that of *development* : a concept empty of everything that forms the peculiar content of history. The old philosophy of history regarded a conceptual working out of history as possible ; either because by introducing the idea of God or of Providence, it read into the facts the aims of a divine intelligence ; or because it treated the formal concept of development as including within itself, logically, the contingent determinations. The case of positivism is strange in that, being neither so boldly imaginative as to yield to the conceptions of teleology and rational philosophy, nor so strictly realistic and intellectually disciplined as to attack the error at its roots, it has halted half way, *i.e.* at the actual concept of development and of evolution, and has announced the philosophy of evolution as the true philosophy of history : development itself—as the law which explains development ! Were this tautology only in question little harm would result ; but the misfortune is that, by a too easy confusion, the concept of evolution often emerges, in the hands of the positivists, from the formal emptiness which belongs to it in truth, and acquires a meaning or rather a pretended meaning, very like the meanings of teleology and metaphysics. The almost religious unction and reverence with which one hears the sacred mystery of *evolution* spoken of gives suffi-cient proof of this.

From such realistic standpoints, now as always, any and every philosophy of history has been criticised. But the very reservations and criticisms of the old mistaken constructions demand a dis-cussion of concepts, that is a process of philoso-phising : although it may be a philosophising which leads properly to the denial of a philosophy of history. Disputes about method, arising out of the needs of the historian, are added. The works published in recent years embody different investi-gations of this kind, and in a plainly realistic sense, under the title of *philosophy of history*. Amongst these I will mention as an example a German pamphlet by Simmel, and, amongst ourselves a compendious introduction by Labriola himself. There are, undoubtedly, still philosophies of his-tory which continue to be produced in the old way : voices *clamantium in deserto*, to whom may be granted the consolation of believing themselves the only apostles of an unrecognised truth.

Now the materialistic theory of history, in the form in which Labriola states it, involves an entire abandonment of all attempt to establish a law of history, to discover a general concept under which all the complex facts of history can be included.

I say 'in the form in which he states it,' because Labriola is aware that several sections of the materialistic school of history tend to approximate to these obsolete ideas.

One of these sections, which might be called that of the *monists*, or *abstract materialists*, is characterised by the introduction of metaphysical materialism into the conception of history.

As the reader knows, Marx, when discussing the relation between his opinions and Hegelianism employed a pointed phrase which has been taken too often beside the point. He said that with Hegel history was standing on its head and that it must be turned right side up again in order to replace it on its feet. For Hegel the idea is the real world, whereas for him (Marx) 'the ideal is nothing else than the material world' reflected and translated by the human mind. Hence the statement so often repeated, that the materialistic view of history is the negation or antithesis of the idealistic view. It would perhaps be convenient to study once again, accurately and critically, these asserted relations between scientific socialism and Hegelianism. To state the opinion which I have formed on the matter ; the link between the two views seems to me to be, in the main, simply *psychological.* Hegelianism was the *early inspiration* of the youthful Marx, and it is natural that everyone should link up the new ideas with the old as a development, an amendment, an antithesis. In fact, Hegel's *Ideas*—and Marx knew this perfectly well—are not human *ideas*, and to turn the Hegelian philosophy of history upside down cannot give us the statement that ideas arise as reflections of material conditions. The inverted form would logically be this : history is not a process of the *Idea*, *i.e.* of a rational reality, but a system of forces : to the rational view is opposed the dynamic view. As to the Hegelian dialectic of concepts it seems to me to bear a purely external and approximate resemblance to the historical notion of economic eras and of the antithetical conditions of society. Whatever may be the value of this suggestion, which I express with hesitation, recognising the difficulty of the problems connected with the interpretation and origin of history ;—this much is evident, that metaphysical materialism, at which Marx and Engels, starting from the extreme Hegelian left, easily arrived, supplied the name and some of the components of their view of history. But both the name and these components are really extraneous to the true character of their conception. This can be neither materialistic nor spiritualistic, nor dualistic nor monadistic : within its limited field the elements of things are not presented in such a way as to admit of a philosophical discussion whether they are reducible one to another, and are united in one ultimate source. What we have before us are concrete objects, the earth, natural production, animals ; we have before us man, in whom the so-called psychical processes appear as differentiated from the so-called physiological processes. To talk in this case of monism and materialism is to talk nonsense. Some socialist writers have expressed surprise because Lange, in his classic *History of Materialism*, does not discuss historical materialism. It is needless to remark that Lange was familiar with Marxian socialism. He was, however, too cautious to confuse the metaphysical materialism with which he was concerned, with historical materialism which has no essential connection with it, and is merely a *way of speaking*.

But the metaphysical materialism of the authors of the new historical doctrine, and the name given to the latter, have been not a little misleading. I will refer as an example to a recent and bad little book, which seems to me symptomatic, by a sufficiently accredited socialist writer, Plechanow.[1] The author, designing to study historical materialism, thinks it needful to go back to Holbach and Helvetius. And he waxes indignant at metaphysical dualism and pluralism, declaring that ' the most important philosophical systems were always *monistic*, that is they interpreted matter and spirit as merely two classes of phenomena having a single and indivisible cause.' And in reference to those who maintain the distinction between the factors in history, he exclaims : ' We see here the old story, always recurring, of the struggle between eclecticism and monism, the story of the dividing walls ; here nature, there spirit, etc.' Many will be amazed at this unexpected leap from the materialistic study

[1] *Beiträge zur Geschichte des Materialismus*, Stuttgart, 1896.

of history into the arms of monism, in which they were unaware that they ought to have such confidence.

Labriola is most careful to avoid this confusion : 'Society is a datum,' he says, 'history is nothing more than the history of society.' And he controverts with equal energy and success the *naturalists*, who wish to reduce the history of man to the history of nature, and the *verbalists*, who claim to deduce from the name materialism the real nature of the new view of history. But it must appear, even to him, that the name might have been more happily chosen, and that the confusion lies, so to speak, inherent in it. It is true that old words can be bent to new meanings, but within limits and after due consideration.

In regard to the tendency to reconstruct a materialistic philosophy of history, substituting an omnipresent Matter for an omnipresent Idea, it suffices to re-assert the impossibility of any such construction, which must become merely superfluous and tautologous unless it abandoned itself to dogmatism. But there is another error, which is remarked among the followers of the materialistic school of history, and which is connected with the former, viz., to anticipate harm not only in the interpretation of history but also in the guidance of practical activities. I refer to the teleological tendencies (abstract teleology), which also Labriola opposes with a cutting attack. The very idea of *progress*, which has seemed to many the only law of history worth saving out of the many devised by philosophical and non-philosophical thinkers, is by him deprived of the dignity of a law, and reduced to a sufficiently narrow significance. The idea of it, says Labriola, is 'not only empirical, but always incidental and hence limited' : progress 'does not influence the sequence of human affairs like destiny or fate, nor like the command of a law.' History teaches us that man is capable of progress ; and we can look at all the different series of events from this point of view : that is all. No less incidental and empirical is the idea of *historical necessity*, which must be freed from all remnants of rationalism and of transcendentalism, so that we see in it the mere recognition of the very small share left in the sequence of events, to individuals and personal free will.

It must be admitted that a little of the blame for the teleological and fatalistic misunderstandings fall on Marx himself. Marx, as he once had to explain, liked to 'coquette' with the Hegelian terminology : a dangerous weapon, with which it would have been better not to trifle. Hence it is now thought necessary to give to several of his statements a somewhat broad interpretation in agreement with the general trend of his theories.[1] Another excuse lies in the impetuous confidence which, as in the case of any practical work, accom-

[1] See, for example, the comments upon some of Marx's statements, in the article *Progrès et développement* in the *Devenir Social* for March, 1896.

panies the practical activities of socialism, and engenders beliefs and expectations which do not always agree with prudent critical and scientific thought. It is strange to see how the positivists, newly converted to socialism, exceed all the others (see the effect of a good school!) in their teleological beliefs, and their facile predeterminations. They swallow again what is worst in Hegelianism, which they once so violently opposed without recognising it. Labriola has finely said that the very forecasts of socialism are merely *morphological* in nature ; and, in fact, neither Marx nor Engels would ever have asserted in the abstract that communism must come about by an unavoidable necessity, in the manner in which they foresaw it. If history is always accidental, why in this western Europe of ours, might not a new barbarism arise owing to the effect of incalculable circumstances? Why should not the coming of communism be either rendered superfluous or hastened by some of those technical discoveries, which, as Marx himself has proved, have hitherto produced the greatest revolutions in the course of history ?

I think then that better homage would be rendered to the materialistic view of history, not by calling it the *final and definite philosophy of history* but rather by declaring that properly speaking *it is not a philosophy of history*. This intrinsic nature which is evident to those who understand it properly, explains the difficulty which exists in finding for it a satisfactory theoretical statement ; and why to Labriola it appears to be only in its beginnings and yet to need much development. It explains too why Engels said (and Labriola accepts the remark), that it is nothing more than a new *method* ; which means a denial that it is a new *theory*. But is it indeed a new method ? I must acknowledge that this name *method* does not seem to me altogether accurate. When the philosophical idealists tried to arrive at the facts of history by inference, this was truly a new method ; and there may still exist some fossil of those blessed times, who makes such attempts at history. But the historians of the materialistic school employ the same intellectual weapons and follow the same paths as, let us say, the philological historians. They only introduce into their work some new *data*, some new *experiences*. The content is different, not the nature of the method.

II

2. *Historical materialism a mass of new data of which historian becomes conscious : Does not state that history is nothing more than economic history, nor does it provide a theory of history : Is simply investigation of influence economic needs have exercised in history : This view does not detract from its importance.*

I HAVE now reached the point which for me is fundamental. Historical materialism is not and cannot be a new philosophy of history or a new method ; but it is properly this ; a *mass of new data, of new experiences*, of which the historian becomes conscious.

It is hardly necessary to mention the overthrow a short time ago of the naïve opinion of the ordinary man regarding the objectivity of history ; almost as though events spoke, and the historian was there to hear and to record their statements. Anyone who sets out to write history has before him documents and narratives, *i.e.* small fragments and traces of what has actually happened. In order to attempt to reconstruct the complete process, he must fall back on a series of assumptions, which are in fact the ideas and information which he possesses concerning the affairs of nature, of man, of society. The pieces needed to complete the whole, of which he has only the fragments before him, he must find within himself. His worth and skill as a historian is shown by the accuracy of his adaptation. Whence it clearly follows that the enrichment of these views and experiences is essential to progress in historical narration.

What are these points of view and experiences which are offered by the materialistic theory of history ?

That section of Labriola's book which discusses this appears to me excellent and sufficient. Labriola points out how historical narration in the course of its development, might have arrived at the theory of *historical factors* ; *i.e.*, the notion that the sequence of history is the result of a number of forces, known as physical conditions, social organisations, political institutions, personal influences. Historical materialism goes beyond, to investigate the interaction of these factors ; or rather it studies them all together as parts of a single process. According to this theory—as is now well known, and as Marx expressed it in a classical passage—the foundations of history are the methods of production, *i.e.* the economic conditions which give rise to class distinctions, to the constitution of rank and of law, and to those beliefs which make up social and moral customs and sentiments, the reflection whereof is found in art, science and religion.

To understand this point of view accurately is not easy, and it is misunderstood by all those who, rather than take it in the concrete, state it absolutely after the manner of an absolute philosophical truth. The theory cannot be maintained in the abstract without destroying it, *i.e.* without turning it into the *theory of the factors*, which is according to my view, the final word in abstract analysis.[1] Some have supposed that historical materialism asserts that history is nothing more than economic history, and all the rest is simply a mask, an appearance without reality. And then they labour to discover the true god of history, whether it be the productive tool or the earth, using arguments which call to mind the proverbial discussion about the egg and the hen. Friedrich Engels was attacked by someone

[1] For this reason I do not, like Labriola, call the theory of the factors a *half-theory* ; nor do I like the comparison with the ancient doctrine, now abandoned in physics, physiology and psychology, of physical forces, vital forces and mental faculties.

who applied to him to ask how the influence of such and such other historical factors ought to be understood in reference to the economic factor. In the numerous letters which he wrote in reply, and which now, since his death, are coming out in the reviews, he let it be understood that, when together with Marx, upon the prompting of the facts, he conceived this new view of history, he had not meant to state an exact theory. In one of these letters he apologises for whatever exaggeration he and Marx may have put into the controversial statements of their ideas, and begs that attention may be paid to the practical applications made of them rather than to the theoretical expressions employed. It would be a fine thing, he exclaims, if a formula could be given for the interpretation of all the facts of history ! By applying this formula, it would be as easy to understand any period of history as to solve a simple equation.[1]

Labriola grants that the supposed reduction of history to the economic factor is a ridiculous notion, which may have occurred to one of the too hasty defenders of the theory, or to one of its no less hasty opponents.[2] He acknowledges the complex-

[1] See a letter dated 21st September 1890, published in the Berlin review, *Der Socialistische Akademiker*, No 19, 1st October 1895. Another, dated 25th January 1894, is printed in No 20, 16th October, of the same review.

[2] He even distinguishes between the *economic interpretation* and the *materialistic view of history*. By the first term he means ' those attempts at analysis, which taking separately on the one hand the economic forms and categories, and on the other for example, law, legislation, politics, custom, proceed to study the

ity of history, how the products of the first degree
first establish themselves, and then isolate themselves and become independent ; the ideals which
harden into traditions, the persistent survivals, the
elasticity of the psychical mechanism which makes
the individual irreducible to a type of his class or
social position, the unconsciousness and ignorance
of their own situations often observed in men, the
stupidity and unintelligibility of the beliefs and sup-
erstitions arising out of unusual accidents and com-
plexities. And since man lives a natural as well as
a social existence, he admits the influence of race, of
temperament and of the promptings of nature.
And, finally, he does not overlook the influence
of the individual, *i.e.* of the work of those who are
called *great men*, who if they are not the creators,
are certainly collaborators of history.

With all these concessions he realises, if I am
not mistaken, that it is useless to look for a theory,
in any strict sense of the word, in historical materialism ; and even that it is not what can properly
be called a *theory* at all. He confirms us in this view
by his fine account of its origin, under the stimulus
of the French Revolution, that great school of
sociology—as he calls it. The materialistic view

mutual influences of the different sides of life, thus abstractly
and subjectively distinguished.' By the second, on the contrary,
' the organic view of history' of the ' totality and unity of social
life,' where economics itself ' is melted into the tide of a process,
to appear afterwards in so many morphological stages, in each
of which it forms the basis relatively to the rest which corresponds to and agrees with it.'

of history arose out of the need to account for a definite social phenomenon, not from an abstract inquiry into the factors of historical life. It was created in the minds of politicians and revolutionists, not of cold and calculating *savants* of the library.

At this stage someone will say :—But if the theory, in the strict sense, is not true, wherein then lies the discovery ? In what does the novelty consist ? To speak in this way is to betray a belief that intellectual progress consists solely in the perfecting of the forms and abstract categories of thought.

Have approximate observations no value in addition to theories ? The knowledge of what has usually happened, everything in short that is called experience of life, and which can be expressed in general but not in strictly accurate terms ? Granting this limitation and understanding always an *almost* and an *about*, there are discoveries to be made which are fruitful in the interpretation of life and of history. Such are the assertions of the dependence of all parts of life upon each other, and of their origin in the economic subsoil, so that it can be said that there is but one single history ; the discovery of the true nature of the State (as it appears in the empirical world), regarded as an institution for the defence of the ruling class ; the proved dependence of ideals upon class interests ; the coincidence of the great epochs of history with the great economic eras ; and the many other observations by which the school of historical materialism is enriched. Always with the aforesaid limitations, it may be said with Engels : ' that men make their history themselves, but within a given limited range, on a basis of conditions actually pre-existent, amongst which the economic conditions, although they may be influenced by the others, the political and ideal, are yet, in the final analysis, decisive, and form the red thread which runs through the whole of history and guides us to an understanding thereof.

From this point of view too, I entirely agree with Labriola in regarding as somewhat strange the inquiries made concerning the supposed forerunners and remote authors of historical materialism, and as quite mistaken the inferences that these inquiries will detract from the importance and originality of the theory. The Italian professor of economics to whom I referred at the beginning, when convicted of a plagiarism, thought to defend himself by saying that, at bottom, Marx's idea was not peculiar to Marx ; hence, at worst, he had robbed a thief. He gave a list of forerunners, reaching back as far as Aristotle. Just lately, another Italian professor reproved a colleague with much less justice for having forgotten that the economic interpretation had been explained by Lorenzo Stein before Marx. I could multiply such examples. All this reminds me of one of Jean Paul Richter's sayings : that we hoard our thoughts as a miser does his money ; and only slowly do we exchange the money for possessions, and thoughts for ex-

periences and feelings. Mental observations attain
real importance through the realisation in thought
and an insight into the fulness of their possibilities.
This realisation and insight have been granted to the
modern socialist movement and to its intellectual
leaders Marx and Engels. We may read even in
Thomas More that the State is a conspiracy of the
rich who make plots for their own convenience :
*quaedam conspiratio divitum, de suis commodis reipub-
licae nomine tituloque tractantium*, and call their
intrigues laws : *machinamenta jam leges fiunt*.[1] And,
leaving Sir Thomas More—who, after all, it will
be said, was a communist—who does not know
by heart Marzoni's lines : *Un' odiosa Forza il mondo
possiede e fa nomarsi Dritto. . . .*[2] But the materialist
and socialist interpretation of the State is not therefore any the less new. The common proverb, indeed,
tells us that interest is the most powerful motive
for human actions and conceals itself under the
most varied forms ; but it is none the less true
that the student of history who has previously
examined the teachings of socialist criticism, is like
a short-sighted man who has provided himself with
a good pair of spectacles : he sees quite differently
and many mysterious shadows reveal their exact
shape.

In regard to historical narrative then, the
materialistic view of history resolves itself into a

---

[1] *Utopia*, L. II (THOMÆ MORI angli *Opera*, Louvain 1566,
f. 18.)

[2] ' Hateful Force rules the world and calls itself Justice.'

warning to keep its observations in mind as a new aid to the understanding of history. Few problems are harder than that which the historian has to solve. In one particular it resembles the problem of the statesman, and consists in *understanding the conditions of a given nation at a given time in respect to their causes and functioning;* but with this difference : the historian confines himself to exposition, the statesman proceeds further to modification ; the former pays no penalty for misunderstanding, whereas the latter is subjected to the severe correction of facts. Confronted by such a problem, the majority of historians—I refer in particular to the conditions of the study in Italy—proceed at a disadvantage, almost like the savants of the old school who constructed philology and researched into etymology. Aids to a closer and deeper understanding, have come at length from different sides, and frequently. But the one which is now offered by the materialistic view of history is great, and suited to the importance of the modern socialist movement. It is true that the historian must render exact and definite in each particular instance, that co-ordination and subordination of factors which is indicated by historical materialism, in general, for the greater number of cases, and approximately ; herein lies his task and his difficulties, which may sometimes be insurmountable. But now the road has been pointed out, along which the solution must be sought, of some of the greatest problems of history apart from those which have been already elucidated.

I will say nothing of the recent attempts at an historical application of the materialistic conception, because it is not a subject to hurry over in passing, and I intend to deal with it on another occasion. I will content myself with echoing Labriola, who gives a warning against a mistake, common to many of these attempts. This consists in retranslating, as he says, into economic phraseology, the old historical perspective which of late has so often been translated into Darwinian phraseology. Certainly it would not be worth while to create a new movement in historical studies in order to attain such a result.

III

3. *Questions as to relation between historical materialism and socialism : Only possible connection lies in special historical application : Bearing of historical materialism upon intellectual and moral truth : Throws light on influence of material conditions on their development, but does not demonstrate their relativity : Absolute morality a necessary postulate of socialism.*

Two things seem to me to deserve some further explanation. What is the relation between historical materialism and socialism ? Labriola, if I am not mistaken, is inclined to connect closely and almost to identify the two things. The whole of socialism lies in the materialistic interpretation of history, which is the truth itself of socialism ; to accept one and reject the other is to understand neither. I consider this statement to be somewhat exaggerated, or, at least, to need explanation. If historical materialism is stripped of every survival of finality and of the benignities of providence, it can afford no apology for either socialism or any other practical guidance for life. On the other hand, in its special historical application, *in the assertion which can be made by its means*, its real and close connection with socialism is to be found. This assertion is as follows :—Society is now so constituted that socialism is the only possible solution which it contains within itself. An assertion and forecast of this kind moreover will need to be filled out before it can be a basis for practical action. It must be completed by motives of interest, or by ethical and sentimental motives, moral judgments and the enthusiasms of faith. The assertion in itself is cold and powerless. It will be insufficient to move the cynic, the sceptic, the pessimist. But it will suffice to put on their guard all those classes of society who see their ruin in the sequence of history and to pledge them to a long struggle, although the final outcome may be useless. Amongst these classes is the proletariat, which indeed aims at the extinction of its class. Moral conviction and the force of sentiment must be added to give positive guidance and to supply an imperative ideal for those who neither feel the blind impulse of class interest, nor allow themselves to be swept along by the whirling current of the times.

The final point which I think demands explanation, although in this case also the difference between myself and Labriola does not appear to be serious, is this : to what conclusions does historical materialism lead in regard to the ideal values of man, in regard that is to intellectual truth and to what is called moral truth ?

The history of the origin of intellectual truth is undoubtedly made clearer by historical materialism, which aims at showing the influence of actual material conditions upon the opening out, and the very development of the human intellect. Thus the history of opinions, like that of science, needs to be for the most part re-written from this point of view. But those who, on account of such considerations concerning historical origins, return in triumph to the old relativity and scepticism, are confusing two quite distinct classes of problem. Geometry owes its origin no doubt to given conditions which are worth determining ; but it does not follow that geometrical truth is something merely historical and relative. The warning seems superfluous, but even here misunderstandings are frequent and remarkable. Have I not read in some socialist author that Marx's *discoveries* themselves are of merely historical *importance* and must necessarily be *disowned*. I do not know what meaning this can have unless it has the very trivial one of a recognition of the limitation of all human work, or unless it resolves itself into the no less idle remark that Marx's thought is the offspring of his age. This onesided history is still more dangerous in reference to moral truth. The science of morality is evidently now in a transformation stage. The ethical imperative, whose classics are Kant's *Kritik der reinen Vernunft*, and Herbart's *Allgemeine praktische Philosophie*, appears no longer adequate. In addition to it an historical and a formal science of morality are making their appearance, which regard morality as a fact, and study its universal nature apart from all preoccupations as to creeds and rules. This tendency shows itself not only in socialistic circles, but also elsewhere, and it will be sufficient for me to refer to Simmel's clever writings. Labriola is thus justified in his defence of new methods of regarding morality. 'Ethics,—he says,—for us resolves itself into an historical study of the subjective and objective conditions according to which morality develops or finds hindrances to its development.' But he adds cautiously, 'in this way alone, *i.e.*, within these limits, is there value in the statement that morality corresponds to the social situation, *i.e.*, *in the final analysis* to the economic conditions.' The question of the intrinsic and absolute worth of the moral ideal, of its reducibility or irreducibility to intellectual truth, remains untouched.

It would perhaps have been well if Labriola had dwelt a little more on this point. A strong tendency is found in socialistic literature towards a moral relativity, not indeed historical, but substantial, which regards morality as a vain imagination. This tendency is chiefly due to the necessity in which

Marx and Engels found themselves, in face of the various types of Utopians, of asserting that the so-called social question is not a moral question,—*i.e.* as this must be interpreted, it cannot be solved by sermons and so-called moral methods—and to their bitter criticism of class ideals and hypocrisies.[1] This result was helped on, as it seems to me, by the Hegelian source of the views of Marx and Engels; it being obvious that in the Hegelian philosophy ethics loses the rigidity given to it by Kant and preserved by Herbart. And lastly the name *materialism* is perhaps not without influence here, since it brings to mind at once well-understood interests and the calculating comparison of pleasures. It is, however, evident that idealism or absolute morality is a necessary postulate of socialism. Is not the interest which prompts the formation of a concept of *surplus-value* a moral interest, or social if it is preferred? Can surplus value be spoken of in pure economics? Does not the labourer sell his labour-power for exactly what it is worth, given his position in existing society? And, without the moral postulate, how could we ever explain Marx's political activity, and that note of violent indignation and bitter satire which is felt in every page of *Das Kapital*? But enough of this, for I find myself making quite elementary statements such

[1] From this point of view it is worth while to note the antipathy which leaks out in socialist writings towards Schiller, the poet of the Kantian morality æsthetically modified, who has become the favourite poet of the German middle classes.

as can only be overlooked owing to ambiguous or exaggerated phraseology.

And in conclusion, I repeat my regret, already expressed, concerning this name *materialism*, which is not justified in this case, gives rise to numerous misunderstandings, and is a cause of derision to opponents. So far as history is concerned, I would gladly keep to the name *realistic view of history*, which denotes the opposition to all teleology and metaphysics within the sphere of history, and combines both the contribution made by socialism to historical knowledge and those contributions which may subsequently be brought from elsewhere. Hence my friend Labriola ought not to attach too much importance, in his serious thoughts, to the adjectives *final and definite*, which have slipped from his pen. Did he not once tell me himself that Engels still hoped for other discoveries which might help us to understand that mystery, made by ourselves, and which is *History* ?

May, 1896.

CHAPTER II. CONCERNING HISTORICAL MATERIALISM VIEWED AS A SCIENCE OF SOCIAL ECONOMICS

1. *Relation between Professor Stammler's book on historical materialism and Marxism : Distinction between pure economics and general historical economics : Socialism not dependent on abstract sociological theory : Stammler's classification of the social sciences : His definition of society : Of social economics : Of social teleology : Nature of Stammler's social science does not provide abstract sociology : Social economics must be either pure economics applied to society or a form of history.*

THE attentive reader of Professor Stammler's book,[1] realises at the outset that it treats of the materialistic theory of history not as a fruitful guide to the interpretation of historical fact, but as a *science* or *philosophy of society.*

A number of attempts have been made, based in the first instance on Marx's statements, to build up on these statements a general theory of history or of society. It is on these attempts then, and not on the least bold amongst them, that Stammler bases his work, making them the starting point of his criticism and reconstruction. It may be precisely

[1] *Wirthschaft und Recht nach der materialistischen Geschichtsauffassung*, eine socialphilosophische Untersuchung, DR RUDOLPH STAMMLER, Professor at the University of Halle, A.S., Leipzig, Veit U.C., 1896, pp. viii–668.

on this account that he chooses to discuss historical materialism in the form given to it by Engels,—which he calls the most complete, the *authentic* (!) statement of the principles of social materialism. He prefers this form to that of Marx, which he thinks too disconnected ; and which is, indeed, less easily reduced to abstract generalities ; whereas Engels was one of the first to give to historical materialism a meaning more important than its original one. To Engels, also, as is well known, is due the very name *materialism* as applied to this view of history.

We cannot, indeed, deny that the materialistic view of history has in fact developed in two directions, distinct *in kind* if not *in practice*, viz. : (1) *a movement relating to the writing of history*, and (2) *a science* and *philosophy of society*. Hence there is no ground for objecting to Stammler's procedure, when he confines himself to this second problem, and takes it up at the point to which he thinks that the followers of historical materialism have brought it. But it should be clearly pointed out that he does not concern himself at all with the problems of historical method. He leaves out of account that is, what, for some people—and for me amongst them—is the side of this movement of thought which is of living and scientific interest.

Professor Stammler remarks how in the propositions employed by the believers in historical materialism : ' *the economic factor dominates the other factors of social life*,' ' *the economic factor is fundamental and the others are dependent,*' and the like, the concept economic has never been defined. He is justified in making this remark, and in attaching the greatest importance to it, if he regards and interprets those propositions as assertions of *laws*, as strict propositions of social science. To use as essential in statements of this kind, a concept which could neither be defined nor explained, and which therefore remained a mere word, would indeed be somewhat odd. But his remark is entirely irrelevant when these propositions are understood as : 'summaries of empirical observations, by the help of which concrete social facts may be explained.' I do not think that any sensible person has ever expected to find in those expressions an accurate and philosophical definition of concepts ; yet all sensible people readily understand to what class of facts they refer. The word *economic* here, as in ordinary language, corresponds, not to a concept, but to a *group* of rather diverse representations, some of which are not even qualitative in content, but quantitative. When it is asserted, that in interpreting history we must look chiefly at the *economic factors*, we think at once of technical conditions, of the distribution of wealth, of classes and sub-classes bound together by definite common interests, and so on. It is true these different representations cannot be reduced to a single concept, but no matter, there is no question of that : here we are in an entirely different *sphere* from that in which abstract questions are discussed.

This point is not without interest and may be explained more in detail. If *economic* be understood in its strict sense, for example, in the sense in which it is employed in pure economics, *i.e.*, if by it be meant the axiom according to which all men seek the greatest satisfaction with the least possible effort, it is plain that to say that this *factor* plays a part (essential, dominant, or equal to that of the others) in social life, would tell us nothing concrete. The economic axiom is a very general and purely a formal principle of conduct. It is inconceivable that any-one should act without applying, well or ill, the very principle of every action, *i.e.*, the economic principle. Worse still if *economic* be taken in the sense which, as we shall see, Professor Stammler gives to it. He understands by this word : 'all concrete social facts ' ; in which sense it would at once become absurd to assert that the economic factor, *i.e.*, *all social facts in the concrete* dominated, a part of these facts ! Thus in order to give a meaning to the word *economic* in this proposition, it is necessary to leave the abstract and formal ; to assign definite ends to human action ; to have in mind an ' historical man,' or rather the average man of history, or of a longer or shorter period of history ; to think, for example, of the need for *bread*, for *clothes*, for *sexual relations*, for the so-called *moral satisfactions*, esteem, vanity, power and so on. The phrase *economic factor* now refers to groups of concrete facts, which are built up in common speech, and which have been better defined from the actual application made of the above-mentioned propositions in historical narrative and in the practical programmes of Marx and his followers.

In the main, this is recognised by Professor Stammler himself when he gives an admirable explanation of the current meaning of the expressions: *economic facts* and *political facts*, revolutions *more political than economic* and vice versa. Such distinctions, he says, can only be understood in the concrete, in reference to the aims pursued by the different sections of society, and to the special problems of social life. According to him, however, Marx's work does not deal with such *trifling matters* : as, for instance, that so-called economic life influences ideas, science, art and so on : old lumber of little consequence. Just as philosophical materialism does not consist in the assertion that bodily facts have an influence over spiritual, but rather in the making of these latter a mere appearance, without reality, of the former : so historical materialism must consist in asserting that economics is the true *reality* and that law is a fallacious *appearance*.

But, with all deference to Professor Stammler, we believe that these *trifling matters*, to which he contemptuously refers, are precisely what are dealt with in Marx's propositions ; and, moreover, we think them neither so trifling nor of such little consequence. Hence Professor Stammler's book does not appear to us a criticism of the most vital part of historical materialism, viz., of a movement or school of historians. The criticism of history is made by history ; and historical materialism is history made or *in the making*.

Nor does it provide the starting point for a criticism of *socialism*, as the programme of a definite social movement. Stammler deceives himself when he thinks that socialism is based on the material-istic philosophy of history as he expounds it : on which philosophy are based, on the contrary, the illusions and caprices of some or of many socialists. Socialism cannot depend on an abstract sociological theory, since the basis would be inadequate pre-cisely because it was abstract ; nor can it depend on a philosophy of history as rhythmical or of little stability, because the basis would be transitory. On the contrary, it is a complex fact and results from different elements ; and, so far as concerns history, socialism does not presuppose a *philosophy of history*, but *an historical conception determined by the existing conditions of society and the manner in which this has come about.* If we put on one side the doc-trines superimposed subsequently, and read again Marx's pages without prejudice, we shall then see that he had, at bottom, no other meaning when he referred to history as one of the factors justifying socialism.

' The necessity for the socialisation of the means of production is not proved scientifically.' Stammler means that the concept of *necessity* as employed by many Marxians, is erroneous ; that the denial of teleology is absurd, and that hence the assertion of the socialisation of the means of production as the social programme is not logically accounted for. This does not hinder this assertion from being possibly quite true. Either because, in addition to

logical demonstrations there are fortunate intui-
tions, or because a conclusion can be true although
derived from a false premiss : it suffices, obviously,
that there should be two errors which cancel one
another. And this would be so in our case. The
denial of teleology ; the tacit acceptance of this
same teleology : here is a method scientifically in-
correct with a conclusion that may be valid. It remains to examine the whole tissue of experiences,
deductions, aspirations and forecasts in which socialism really consists ; and over which Stammler
passes indifferently, content to have brought to
light an error in the philosophical statement of a
remote postulate, an error which some, or it may
be many, of the supporters and politicians of socialism commit.

All these reservations are needed in order to
fix the scope of Stammler's investigation ; but it
would be a mistake to infer from them that we reject the starting point of the inquiry itself. Historical materialism—says Professor Stammler—has
proved unable to give us a valid *science of society* :
we, however, believe that this was not its main or
original object. The two statements come practically to the same thing : the science of society is
not contained in the literature of the materialistic
theory. Professor Stammler adds that although
historical materialism does not offer an acceptable
social theory, it nevertheless gives a *stimulus of the
utmost intensity* towards the formation of such a
theory. This seems to us a matter of merely individual psychology : suggestions and stimuli, as

everyone knows, differ according to the mind that receives them. The literature of historical materialism has always aroused in us a desire to study history in the concrete, *i.e.*, to reconstruct the actual historical process. In Professor Stammler, on the contrary, it arouses a desire to throw aside this meagre empirical history, and to work with abstractions in order to establish concepts and general points of view. The problems which he sets before himself, might be arrived at psychologically by many other paths.

There is a tendency, at present, to enlarge unduly the boundaries of social studies. But Stammler rightly claims a definite and special subject for what ought to be called *social science* ; that is *definite social data*. Social science must include nothing which has not *sociability* as its determining cause. How can ethics ever be social science, since it is based on cases of conscience which evade all social rules ? *Custom* is the social fact, not *morality*. How can *pure economics* or *technology* ever be social science, since those concepts are equally applicable to the isolated individual and to societies ? Thus in studying *social data* we shall see that, considered in general, they give rise to two distinct theories. The first theory regards the concept *society* from the *causal* standpoint ; the second regards it from the *teleological* standpoint. Causality and teleology cannot be substituted the one for the other ; but one forms the complement of the other.

If, then, we pass from the general and abstract to the concrete, we have society as existing in history. The study of the facts which develop in concrete society Stammler consigns to a science which he calls *social* (or *political*, or *national*) *economics*. From such facts may still be abstracted the mere form, *i.e.*, the collection of rules supplied by history by which they are governed ; and this may be studied independently of the matter. Thus we get *jurisprudence*, or the technical science of law ; which is always bound up inseparably with a given actual historical material, which it works up by scientific method, endeavouring to give it unity and coherence. Finally, amongst social studies are also included those investigations which aim at judging and determining whether a given social order is as it ought to be ; and whether attempts to preserve or change it are objectively justified. This section may be called that of practical social problems. By such definitions and divisions Professor Stammler exhausts every possible form of social study. Thus we should have the following scheme :

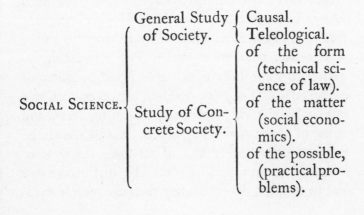

SOCIAL SCIENCE.

General Study of Society.
{ Causal.
{ Teleological.

Study of Concrete Society.
{ of the form (technical science of law).
{ of the matter (social economics).
{ of the possible, (practical problems).

We believe that this table correctly represents his views, although given in our own way, and in words somewhat different from those used by him. A new treatment of the social sciences, the work of serious and keen ability, such as Stammler seems to possess, cannot fail to receive the earnest attention of all students of a subject which is still so vague and controversial. Let us examine it then section by section.

The first investigation relating to society, that concerned with causality, would be directed to solving the problem of the *nature* of society. Many definitions have been given of this up to the present : and none of them can be said to be generally accepted, or even to claim wide support. Stammler indeed, rejects, after criticism, the definitions of Spencer or Rümelin, which appear to him to be the most important and to be representative of all the others. Society is not an *organism* (Spencer), nor is it merely something opposed to *legalised society* (Rümelin) : Society, says Stammler, is ' *life lived by men in common, subject to rules which are externally binding.*' These rules must be understood in a very wide sense, as all those which bind men living together to something which is satisfied by outward performance. They are divided, however, into two large classes : rules properly speaking *legal*, and rules of *convention*. The second class includes the precepts of propriety and of custom, the code of knightly honour, and so on. The distinctive test lies in the fact that the latter class are merely *hypo-*

thetical, while the former are imposed without being desired by those subjected to them. The whole assemblage of rules, legal and conventional, Stammler calls social *form.* Under these rules, obeying them, limiting them and even breaking them men act in order to satisfy their desires ; in this, and in this alone, human life consists. The assemblage of concrete facts which men produce when working together in society, *i.e.*, under the assumption of social rules, Stammler calls *social matter*, or *social economics.* Rules, and actions under rules ; these are the two elements of which every social datum consists. If the rules were lacking, we should be outside society ; we should be animals or gods, as says the old proverb : if the actions were lacking there would remain only an empty form, built up hypothetically by thought, and no portion of which was actually real. Thus social life appears as a single fact : to separate its two constituent factors means either to destroy it, or to reduce it to empty form. The law governing changes within society cannot be found in something which is extra social ; not in technique and discovery, nor in the workings of supposed natural laws, nor in the influence of great men, of mysterious racial and national spirit ; but it must be sought in the very centre of the social fact itself. Hence it is wrong to speak of a causal bond between law and economics or vice versa : the relation between law and economics is that between the rule and the things ruled, not one of cause and effect. The determining cause of social movements and changes is then ultimately to be found in the actual working out of social rules, which precede such changes. This concrete working out, these actions accomplished under rules, may produce (1) social mutations which are entirely *quantitative* (in the number of social facts of one or another kind) ; (2) mutations which are also *qualitative*, consisting that is in changes in the rules themselves. Hence the *circle of social life* : rules, social facts arising under them ; ideas, opinions, desires, efforts resulting from the facts ; changes in the rules. When and how this circle originated, that is to say when and how social life arose on the earth, is a question for history, which does not concern the theorist. Between social life and non-social life there are no gradations, theoretically there is a gulf. But as long as social life exists, there is no escape from the circle described above.

The form and matter of social life thus come into conflict, and from this conflict arises change. By what test can the issue of the conflict be decided ? To appeal to facts, to invent a causal necessity which may agree with some ideal necessity is absurd. In addition to the law of social *causality*, which has been expounded, there must be a law of ends and ideals, *i.e.*, a *social teleology*. According to Stammler, historical materialism identifies, nor would it be the only theory to attempt such an identification, *causality* and *teleology* ; but it, too, cannot escape from the logical contradictions which such assertions contain. Much praise has been given to that section of Professor Stammler's book in which he shows how teleological assumptions are constantly implied by historical materialism in all its assertions of a practical nature. But we confess that the discovery seems to us exceedingly easy, not to be compared to that of Columbus about the egg. Here again we must point out that the *pivot* of the Marxian doctrine lies in the *practical problem* and not in the *abstract theory*. The denial of finality is, at bottom, the denial of a merely subjective and peculiar finality. And here, too, although the criticism as applied to historical materialism seems to us hardly accurate, we agree with Stammler's conclusion, *i.e.*, that it is necessary to construct, or better to reconstruct, with fresh material, a theory of social teleology.

Let us omit, for the present, an examination of Stammler's construction of teleology, which includes some very fine passages (*e.g.* the criticism of the anarchist doctrine) and ask instead : What is this social science of Stammler, of which we have stated the striking and characteristic features ? The reader will have little difficulty in discovering that the second investigation, that concerning social teleology, is nothing but a modernised *philosophy of law*. And the first ? Is it that long desired and hitherto vainly sought *general sociology* ? Does it give us a new and acceptable concept of society ? To us it appears evident that the first investigation is nothing but a *formal science of law*. In it Professor Stammler studies *law as a fact*, and hence he cannot find it except in *society subjected to rules imposed from without*. In the second, he studies law as an *ideal* and constructs the philosophy (imperative) of law. We are not here questioning the *value* of the investigation, but its *nature*. The present writer is convinced that social data leave no place for an abstract independent science. Society is a *living together* ; the kind of phenomena which appear in this life together is the concern of descriptive history. But it is perfectly possible to study this life together from a given point of view, *e.g.*, from the legal point of view, or, in general, from that of the legal and non-legal rules to which it can be subjected ; and this Stammler has done. And, in so doing, he has examined the nature of law, separating the concrete individual laws and the ideal type of law ; which he has then studied apart. This is the reason why Stammler's investigation seems to us a truly scientific investigation and very well carried out, but not an abstract and general science *of society*. Such a science is for us inconceivable, just as a formal science of law is, on the contrary, perfectly conceivable.

As to the second investigation, that concerning teleology, there would be some difficulty in including it in the number of sciences if it be admitted that ideals are not subjects for science. But here Professor Stammler himself comes to our assistance by assigning the foundation of social teleology to philosophy, which he defines as the science of the True and of the Good, the science of the Absolute, and understands in a non-formal sense.

Professor Stammler speaks readily of a *monism* of the social life, and accepts as suitable and accurate the name *materialism* as applied to Marx's conception of history, and connects this *materialism* with metaphysical materialism, applying to it also Lange's statement, viz., that 'materialism may be the first and lowest step of philosophy, but it is also the most substantial and solid.' For him historical materialism offers truth, but not the whole truth, since it regards as real the *matter* only and not the *form* of social life ; hence the necessity of completing it by restoring the *form* to its place, and fixing the relation between *form* and *matter*, combining the two in the unity of *social life*. We doubt whether Engels and his followers ever understood the phrase *social materialism* in the sense which Stammler assigns to it. The parallel drawn between it and metaphysical materialism seems to us somewhat arbitrary.

We come to the group of concrete sciences, *i.e.*, those which have for their subject society as given in history. No one who has had occasion to consider the problem of the classification of the sciences, will be inclined to give the character of independent and autonomous sciences to studies of the practical problems of this or that society, and to jurisprudence, and the technical study of law. This latter is only an interpretation or explanation of a given existing legal system, made either for practical reasons, or as simple historical knowledge. But what we think merits attention more than these questions of terminology and classification, is the conception of *social economics*, advanced by Stammler ; of the second, that is, of the concrete social sciences, enumerated above. The difficulties arising out of this conception are more serious, and centre on the following points ; whether it is a new and valid conception, or whether it should be reduced to something already known ; or finally whether it is not actually erroneous.

Stammler holds forth at length against economics regarded as a science in itself, which has its own laws and which has its source in an original and irreducible economic principle. It is a mistake, he says, to put forward an abstract economic science and subdivide it into economic science relating to the individual and social economic science. There is no ground of union between these two sciences, because the economics of the isolated individual offers us only concepts which are dealt with by the natural sciences and by technology, and is nothing but an assemblage of simple natural observations, explained by means of physiology and individual psychology. Social economics, on the other hand, offers the peculiar and characteristic conditions of the *externally binding rules*, under which activities develop. And what can an economic principle be if not a hypothetical maxim : the man who wishes to secure this or that object of subjective satisfaction must employ these or those means, ' a maxim which is more or less generally obeyed, and sometimes violated ' ? The dilemma lies then between the natural and technological consideration and the social one : *there is no third thing.* '*Ein Drittes ist nicht da !*' This Stammler frequently reiterates, and always in the same words. But the dilemma (whose unfortunate inspiration he owes to Kant) does not hold, it is a case of a trilemma. Besides the concrete social facts, and besides the technological and natural knowledge, there is a third thing, viz., the economic principle, or hedonistic postulate, as it is preferred to call it. Stammler asserts that this third thing is not *equal in value* to the two first ones, that it comes as a *secondary* consideration, and we confess that we do not clearly understand what this means. What he ought to prove is that this principle *can be reduced* to the two former ones, viz., to the technical or to the social conditions. This he has not done, and indeed we do not know how it could be done. That economics, thus understood, is not social science, we are so much the more inclined to agree since he himself says as much in calling it *pure* economics, *i.e.*, something built up by abstraction from particular facts and hence also from the social fact. But this does not mean that it is not applicable to society, and cannot give rise to inferences in *social economics*. The social factor is then assumed as a medium through which the economic principle displays its influence and produces definite results. Granted the economic principle, and granted, for example, the legal regulation of private property in land, and the existence of land differing in quality, and granted other conditions, then the fact of rent of land arises of necessity. In this and other like examples, which could easily be brought forward, we have laws of social and political economics, *i.e.*, deductions from the economic principle acting under given legal conditions. It is true that, under other legal conditions, the effects would be different ; but none of the effects would occur were it not for the economic nature of man, which is a necessary postulate, and not to be identified with the postulate of technical knowledge, or with any other of the social rules. *To know* is not to *will* ; and *to will in accordance with objective rules* is not *to will in accordance with ideals which are merely subjective and individual* (economic).

Stammler might say that if the science of economics thus interpreted is not properly a social science, he leaves it on one side, because his object is to construct a science which may be fully entitled to the name of *social economics*. But—let us, too, construct a dilemma !—this social economics, to which he aspires, will either be just economic science applied to definite social conditions, in the sense now indicated, or it will be a form of historical knowledge. No third thing exists. *Ein Drittes ist nicht da!*

And indeed, for Stammler an *economic phenomenon* is not any single social fact whatever, but a group of homogeneous facts, which offer the marks of *necessity*. The number of economic facts required to form the group and give rise to an economic phenomenon cannot be determined in general ; but can be seen in each case. By the formation of these groups, he says, social economics does not degenerate into a register of data concerning fact, nor does it become purely mechanical statistics of material already given which it has merely to enumerate. Social economics should not merely examine into the change in the actual working out of one and the same social order, but remains, now as formerly, the seat of all knowledge of actual social life. It must start from the knowledge of a given social existence, both in regard to its form and in regard to its content ; and enlarge and deepen it up to the most minute peculiarity of its actual working out, with the accuracy of a technical science, the conditions and concrete objects of which are clearly indicated ; and thus free the reality of social life from every obscurity. Hence it must make for itself a series of concepts, which will serve the purpose of such an explanation.

Now this account of the concept of *social economics* is capable of two interpretations. The first is that it is intended to describe a science, which has indeed for its object (as is proper for sciences) *necessary* connections, in the strict sense of the word. But how establish this *necessity* ? How make the concepts suitable to *social economics* ? Evidently by allowing ourselves to be guided by a principle, by abstracting a single side from concrete reality ; and if it is to be for economics this principle can be none other than the *economic principle*, and social economics will consider only the economic side of a given social life. Profits, rent, interest, labour value, usury, wages, crises, will then appear as economic phenomena necessary under given conditions of the social order, through which the economic principle exerts its influence.

The other interpretation is that Stammler's social economics does not indeed accomplish the dissolving work of analysis but considers this or that social life in the concrete. In this case it could do nothing but *describe* a given society. To *describe* does not mean to *describe in externals and superficially* ; but, more accurately, to free that group of facts from every obscurity, showing what it actually is, and describing it, as far as possible in its naked reality. But this is, in fact, historical knowledge, which may assume varied forms, or rather may define in various ways its own subject. It may study a *society*—in all its aspects during a given period of time, or at a given moment of its existence, or it may even take up one or more aspects of social life and study them as they present themselves in different societies and at different times, and so on. It is history always, even when it avails itself of *comparison* as an instrument of research. And such a study will not have to make *concepts*, but will take them as it needs them from those sciences, which do, in fact, elaborate concepts.

Thus it would have been of great interest to see the working out of this new *social economics* of Stammler a little more clearly, so that we might determine exactly in which of the aforesaid two classes it ought to be placed. Whether it is merely political economy in the ordinary sense, or whether it is the concrete study of single societies and of groups of them. In the latter case Stammler has added another name or rather two names ; *science of the matter of social life* and *social economics*, to the many phrases by which of late the old *History* has been disguised (social history, history of civilisation, concrete sociology, comparative sociology, psychology of the populace and of the classes, etc.). And the gain, if we may be allowed to say so, will not be great.

September 1898.

CHAPTER III. CONCERNING THE INTER-PRETATION AND CRITICISM OF SOME CONCEPTS OF MARXISM

I

OF THE SCIENTIFIC PROBLEM IN MARX'S 'DAS KAPITAL'

Das Kapital an abstract investigation : His society is not this or that society : Treats only of capitalist society : Assumption of equivalence between value and labour : Varying views about meaning of this law : Is a postulate or standard of comparison : Question as to value of this standard : Is not a moral ideal : Treats of economic society in so far as is a working society : Shows special way in which problem is solved in capitalist society : Marx's deductions from it.

NOTWITHSTANDING the many expositions, criticisms, summaries and even abbreviated extracts in little works of popular propaganda, which have been made of Karl Marx's work, it is far from easy, and demands no small effort of philosophical and abstract thought, to understand the exact nature of the investigation which Marx carried out. In addition to the intrinsic difficulty of the subject, it does not appear that the author himself always realised fully the peculiar character of his investigation, that is to say its theoretical distinctness from all other investigations which may be made with his economic material ; and, throughout, he despised and neglected all such preliminary and exact explanations as might have made his task plain. Then, moreover, account must be taken of the strange composition of the book, a mixture of general theory, of bitter controversy and satire, and of historical illustrations or digressions, and so arranged that only Loria, (fortunate man !), can declare *Das Kapital* to be the *finest and most symmetrical* of existing books ; it being, in reality, unsymmetrical, badly arranged and out of proportion, sinning against all the laws of good taste ; resembling in some particulars Vico's *Scienza nuova*. Then too there is the Hegelian phraseology beloved by Marx, of which the tradition is now lost, and which, even within that tradition he adapted with a freedom that at times seems not to lack an element of mockery. Hence it is not surprising that *Das Kapital* has been regarded, at one time or another, as an economic treatise, as a philosophy of history, as a collection of sociological laws, so-called, as a moral and political book of reference, and even, by some, as a bit of narrative history.

Nevertheless the inquirer who asks himself what is the *method* and what the *scope* of Marx's investigation, and puts on one side, of course, all the historical, controversial and descriptive portions (which certainly form an organic part of the book but not of the fundamental investigation), can at once reject most of the above-mentioned definitions, and decide clearly these two points :

(1) As regards *method*, *Das Kapital* is without doubt an *abstract* investigation ; the capitalist society studied by Marx, is not this or that society, historically existing, in France or in England, nor the modern society of the most civilised nations, that of Western Europe and America. It is an ideal and formal society, deduced from certain hypotheses, which could indeed never have occurred as actual facts in the course of history. It is true that these hypotheses correspond to a great extent to the historical conditions of the modern civilised world ; but this, although it may establish the importance and interest of Marx's investigation because the latter helps us to an understanding of the workings of the social organisms which closely concern us, does not alter its nature. Nowhere in the world will Marx's categories be met with as living and real existences, simply because they are abstract categories, which, in order to live must lose some of their qualities and acquire others.

(2) As regards *scope*, Marx's investigation does not cover the whole field of economic fact, nor even that one ultimate and dominant portion, whence all economic facts have their source, like rivers flowing from a mountain. It limits itself, on the contrary, to one special economic system, that which occurs in a society with private property in

capital, or, as Marx says, in the phrase peculiar to him, *capitalist*. There remained untouched, not only the other systems which have existed in history and are possible in theory, such as monopolist society, or society with collective capital, but also the series of economic phenomena common to the different societies and to individual economics. To sum up, as regards *method*, *Das Kapital* is not an historical description, and as regards *scope*, it is not an economic *treatise*, much less an *encyclopedia*.

But, even when these two points are settled, the real essence of Marx's investigation is not yet explained. Were *Das Kapital* nothing but what we have so far defined, it would be merely an *economic monograph on the laws of capitalist society*.[1] Such a monograph Marx could only have made in one way : by deciding on these laws, and explaining them by general laws, or by the fundamental concepts of economics ; by reducing, in short, the complex to the simple, or passing, by deductive reasoning, and with the addition of fresh hypotheses, from the simple to the complex. He would thus have shown, by precise exposition, how the apparently most diverse facts of the economic world are ultimately governed by one and the

[1] 'An immense monograph' (of economics understood) it is called by Professor Antonio Labriola, the most notable of the Italian Marxians, in his recent book (*Discorrendo di filosophia e socialismo*, Rome, Loescher, 1898). But in an earlier work (*In Memoria del 'Manifesto dei Comunisti'*, 2nd ed. Rome, 1895, p. 36) he defined it as '*a philosophy of history*'.

same law ; or, what is the same thing, how this law is differently refracted as it takes effect through different organisations, without changing itself, since otherwise the means and indeed the test of the explanation would be lacking. Work of this nature had been already carried out, to a great extent, in Marx's time, and since then it has been developed yet further by economists, and has attained a high degree of perfection, as may be seen, for instance, in the economic treatises of our Italian writers, Pantaleoni and Pareto. But I much doubt whether Marx would have become an economist in order to devote himself to a species of research of almost solely theoretical, or even scholastic, interest. His whole personality as a practical man and a revolutionist, impatient of abstract investigation which had no close connection with the interests of actual life, would have recoiled from such a course. If *Das Kapital* was to have been merely an economic monograph, it would be safe to wager that it would never have come into existence.

What then did Marx accomplish, and to what treatment did he subject the phenomena of capitalist society, if not to that of pure economic theory ? *Marx assumed, outside the field of pure economic theory, a proposition ; the famous equivalence between value and labour ; i.e. the proposition that the value of the commodities produced by labour is equal to the quantity of labour socially necessary to produce them.* It is only with this assumption that his special investigation begins.

But what connection has this proposition with the laws of capitalist society? or what part does it play in the investigation? This Marx never explicitly states; and it is on this point that the greatest confusions have arisen, and that the interpreters and critics have been most at a loss.

Some of them have explained the law of labour-value as an *historical* law, peculiar to capitalist society, all of whose manifestions it determines;[1] others rightly seeing that the manifestations of capitalist society are by no means determined by such a law, but comply with the general economic motives characteristic of the economic nature of man, have rejected the law as an absurdity at which Marx arrived by pressing to its extreme consequences an unfortunate concept of Ricardo.

Criticism was thus bewildered between entire acceptance, combined with a clearly erroneous interpretation, and entire and summary rejection of Marx's treatment; until, in recent years, and especially after the appearance of the third and posthumous volume of *Das Kapital*, it began to seek out and follow a better path. In truth, despite its eager defenders, the Marxian doctrine has always remained obscure; and, despite contemptuous and

---

[1] I leave out those who regard the law of labour-value as the *general* law of value. The refutation is obvious. How could it ever be 'general' when it leaves out of account a whole category of economic goods, that is the goods which cannot be increased by labour?

summary condemnation, it has always displayed also an obstinate vitality not usually possessed by nonsense and sophistry. For this reason it is to the credit of Professor Werner Sombart, of Breslau University, that he has declared, in one of his lucid writings, that Marx's practical conclusions may be refuted from a political standpoint, but that, scientifically, it is above all important to *understand* his ideas.[1]

Sombart, then, breaking openly with the interpretation of Marx's law of value as a *real* law of economic phenomena, and giving a fuller, and I may say, a bolder expression to the timid opinions already stated by another (C. Schmidt), says, that *Marx's law of value* is not *an empirical but a conceptual fact* (Keine empirische, sondern eine gedankliche Thatsache) ; that Marx's value is a *logical fact* (eine logische Thatsache), which aids our thought in understanding the actual realities of economic life.[2]

This interpretation, in its general sense, was accepted by Engels, in an article written some months before his death and published posthumously. To Engels it appeared that 'it could not be condemned as inaccurate, but that, nevertheless,

---

[1] WERNER SOMBART : *Zur Kritik des oekonomischer Systems von Karl Marx* (in the *Archiv fur soziale Gesetzgebung und Statistik* Vol. VII, 1894, pp. 555-594). I have not by me the criticism (from the Hedonistic point of view) of this article by Sombart—on the third volume of *Das Kapital*—made last year by BOHM BAWERK in the *Miscellany* in honour of Knies.

[2] *Loc. cit.,* p. 571, *et seq.*

it was too vague and might be expressed with greater precision.' [1]

The acute and courteous remarks on the theory of value, published lately in an article in the *Journal des Economistes* by an able French Marxian, Sorel, indicate a movement in the same direction. In these remarks he acknowleges that there is no way of passing from Marx's theory to actual phenomena of economic life, and that, although it may offer elucidation, in a somewhat limited sense, it does not appear further that it could ever *explain*, in the scientific meaning of the word. [2]

And now too Professor Labriola, in a hasty glance at the same subject, referring clearly to Sombart, and partly agreeing and partly criticising, writes : 'the theory of value does not denote an empirical *factum* nor does it express a merely *logical proposition*, as some have imagined ; but it is the *typical premise* without which all the rest would be unthinkable.' [3]

Labriola's phrase appears to me, in fact, somewhat more accurate than Sombart's ; who, moreover, shows himself dissatisfied with his own term, like someone who has not yet a quite definite concept in view, and hence cannot find a satisfactory phrase.

---

[1] In the *Neue Zeit* xiv. vol. 1, pp. 4-11, 37-44, I quote from the Italian translation : *Dal terzo volume del ' Capitale,'* preface and notes by F. Engels, Rome 1896, p. 39.

[2] *Sur la théorie Marxiste de la valeur* (in the *Journal des Economistes*, number for March 1897, pp. 222-31, see p. 228).

[3] *Discorrendo di socialismo e di filosophia*, p. 21.

'*Conceptual fact*,' '*logical fact*' expresses much too little since it is evident that all sciences are interwoven from logical facts, that is from concepts. Marx's labour-value is not only a logical generalisation, it is also *a fact conceived and postulated as typical*, i.e. something more than a mere logical concept. Indeed it has not the inertia of the abstract but the force of a concrete fact,[1] which has in regard to capitalist society, in Marx's investigation, the function of a term of comparison, of a standard, of a *type*.[2]

This standard or type being postulated, the investigation, for Marx, takes the following form. Granted that value is equal to the labour socially necessary, it is required to show *with what divergencies from this standard* the prices of commodities are fixed in capitalist society, and how labour-power itself acquires a price and becomes a commodity. To speak plainly, Marx stated the problem in unappropriate language ; he represented this typical value itself, postulated by him as a standard, as being the *law* governing the economic phenomena of capitalist society. And it is the law, if he likes,

---

[1] It must be carefully noticed that what I call a *concrete fact* may still not be a fact which is empirically real, but a fact made by us hypothetically and *entirely imaginary*, or a fact *partially empirical*, i.e. existing partially in empirical reality. We shall see later on that Marx's typical premise belongs properly to this second class.

[2] I accept the term employed by Labriola so much the more readily since it is the same as that used by me a year ago. See Essay on Loria (*Materialismio Storico*, pp. 48-50).

but in the *sphere of his conceptions*, not *in economic reality*. We may conceive the divergencies from a standard as the revolt of reality when confronted by this standard which we have endowed with the dignity of law.

From a formal point of view there is nothing absurd about the investigation undertaken by Marx. It is a usual method of scientific analysis to regard a phenomenon not only as it exists, but also as it would be if one of its factors were altered, and, in comparing the hypothetical with the real phenomenon, to conceive the first as diverging from the second, which is postulated as fundamental, or the second as diverging from the first, which is postulated in the same manner. If I build up by deductive reasoning the moral rules which develop in two social groups which are at war one against another, and if I show how they differ from the moral rules which develop in a state of peace, I should be making something *analogous* to the comparison worked out by Marx. Nor would there be great harm (although the expression would be neither fortunate nor accurate) in saying, in a figurative sense, that the *law* of the moral rules in time of war is the same as that of the rules in time of peace, modified to the new conditions, and altered in a way which seems, ultimately, inconsistent with itself. As long as he confines himself to the limits of his hypothesis Marx proceeds quite correctly. Error could come in only when he or others confuse the hypothetical with the real, and the manner of conceiving and of judging with that of existing. As long as this mistake is avoided, the method is unassailable.

But the formal justification is insufficient : we need another. With a formally correct method results may be obtained which are meaningless and unimportant, or mere mental tricks may be performed. To set up an arbitrary standard of comparison, to compare, and deduce, and to end by establishing a series of divergencies from this standard ; to what will this lead ? It is then, the *standard itself* which needs justification : *i.e.* we need to decide what meaning and importance it may have for us.

This question too, although not stated exactly in this way, has occurred to Marx's critics ; and an answer to it has been already given some time ago and by many, by saying that the equivalence of value and labour is an ideal of social ethics, a *moral ideal*. But nothing could be imagined more mistaken in itself and farther from Marx's thought than this interpretation. What moral inference can ever be drawn from the premiss that value is equal to the labour socially necessary ? If we reflect a little, *absolutely none*. The establishment of this fact tells us nothing about the needs of the society, which needs will make necessary one or another ethical-legal system of property and of methods of distribution. Value may certainly equal labour, nevertheless special historical conditions will make necessary society organised in castes or in classes, divided into governing and governed, rulers and ruled ; with a resulting unequal distribution of the products of labour. Value may certainly equal labour ; but even supposing that fresh historical conditions ever make possible the disappearance of society organised in classes and the advent of a communistic society, and even supposing that in this society distribution could take place according to the quantity of labour contributed by each person, this distribution would still not be a deduction from the established equivalence between value and labour, but a standard adopted for special reasons of social convenience.[1] Nor can it be said that such an equivalence supplies in itself an idea of perfect justice (even though unrealisable), since the criterion of justice has no relation to the difference often due to purely natural causes, in the ability to do more or less social labour and to produce a greater or smaller value. Thus neither a rule of abstract justice nor one of convenience and social utility can be derived from the equivalence between value and labour. Rules of either kind can only be based on consideration of a quite different grade from that of a simple economic equation.

[1] In making an hypothesis of this nature, Marx distinguished clearly that, in such a case, ' labour-time would serve a *double* purpose : on the one hand as standard of value, on the other as a standard of the individual share reckoned to each producer in the common labour ' (*andrerseits dient die Arbeitzeit zugleich als Mass des individuellen Antheils des Producenten an der Gemeinarbeit, und daher auch an dem individuell verzehbaren Theil des Gemein products*) : See *Das Kapital* I, p. 45.

Sombart, avoiding this vulgar confusion, has been better advised in looking for the meaning of the standard set up by Marx in the nature of society itself, and apart from our moral judgments. Thus he says that labour is *the economic fact of greater objective importance*, and that value, in Marx's view, is nothing 'if not the economic expression of the fact of the socially productive power of labour, as the basis of economic existence.'

But this investigation appears to me to be merely begun and not yet worked out to a conclusion; and if I might suggest wherein it needs completion, I should remark that it is necesary to attempt to give clearness and precision to this word *objective*, which is either ambiguous or metaphorical. What is meant by an economically objective fact? Do not these words suggest rather a mere *presentiment of a concept* instead of the distinct vision of this concept itself?

I will add, merely tentatively, that the word *objective* (whose correlative term is *subjective*) does not seem to be in place here. Let us, instead, take account, in a society, only of what is properly economic life, *i.e.* out of the whole society, only of *economic society*. Let us abstract from this latter all goods which cannot be increased by labour. Let us abstract further all class distinctions, which may be regarded as accidental in reference to the general concept of economic society. Let us leave out of account all modes of distributing the wealth produced, which, as we have said, can only be determined on grounds of convenience or perhaps of justice, but in anycase upon considerations belonging to society as a whole, and never from considertions belonging exclusively to economic society. What is left after these successive abstractions have been made? Nothing but *economic society in so far as it is a working society.*[1] And in this society without class distinctions, *i.e.* in an economic society as such and whose only commodities are the products of labour, what can value be? Obviously the sum of the efforts, *i.e.* the quantity of labour, which the production of the various kinds of commodities demands. And, since we are here speaking of the economic social organism, and not of the individual persons living in it, it follows that this labour cannot be reckoned except by averages, and hence as labour *socially* (it is with society, I repeat, that we are here dealing) *necessary.*

Thus labour-value would appear as that determination of value peculiar to economic society as such, when regarded only in so far as it produces commodities capable of being increased by labour.

From this definition the following corollary may be drawn : the determination of labour value *will have a positive conformity with facts as long as a society exists, which produces goods by means of labour.* It is evident that in the imaginary county of Cocaigne this determination would have no con-

---

[1] This is a different thing from the workmen or operatives in our capitalist society, who form a *class*, *i.e.* a portion of economic society and not economic society in general and in the abstract, producing goods which can be increased by labour.

formity with facts, since all goods would exist in quantities exceeding the demand ; similarly it is also evident that the same determination could not take effect in a society in which goods were inadequate to the demand, but could not be increased by labour.

But hitherto history has shown us only societies which, in addition to the enjoyment of goods not increasable by labour, have satisfied their needs by labour. Hence this equivalence between value and labour has hitherto had and will continue for an indefinite time to have, a conformity with facts ; but, of what kind is this conformity ? Having ruled out (1) that it is a question of a moral ideal, and (2) that it is a question of scientific law ; and having nevertheless concluded that this equivalence is a *fact* (which Marx uses as a type), we are obliged to say, as the only alternative, that *it is a fact, but a fact which exists in the midst of other facts ; i.e. a fact that appears to us empirically as opposed, limited, distorted by other facts,* almost like a force amongst other forces, which produces a resultant different from what it would produce if the other forces ceased to act. *It is not a completely dominant fact but neither is it non-existent and merely imaginary.*[1]

---

[1] It may be doubted whether this general application of labour-value to every working economic society was included in the ideas of Marx and Engels, when the numerous passages are recalled in which one or other has declared many times that *in the future communistic society the criterion of value will disappear and production will be based on social utility,* cf. Engels as

It is still necessary to remark that in the course of history this *fact* has undergone various alterations, *i.e.*, has been more or less obscured ; and here it is proper to do justice to Engels' remark in reference to Sombart ; that as regards the way in which the latter defines the law of value ' he does not bring out the full importance which this law possesses during the stages of economic development in which it is supreme.' Engels makes a digression into the field of economic history to show that Marx's law of value, *i.e.* the equivalence between value and the labour socially necessary, has been supreme for several thousand years.[1] Supreme is too strong a term ; but it is true that the opposed influences of other facts to this law have been fewer in number and less intense under primitive communism and under mediæval and domestic economic conditions, whilst they have reached a maximum in the society based on priv-

early as in the *Umrisse* 1844, (Italian translation in *Critica sociale* a. v. 1895) *Marx, Misère de la philosophie*, 2nd ed. Paris, Giard et Brière. 1896, p. 83 ; Engels *Antidühring*, p. 335. But this must be understood in the sense that, not being a hypothetical communistic society based on exchange, the function of value (in exchange) would lose, according to them, its practical importance ; but not in the other sense that in the opinion of the communistic society the value of goods would no longer equal the labour which they cost to society. Because even in such a system of economic organisation, value-labour would be the economic law which entirely governed the valuation of individual commodities, produced by labour. There would be that clearness of valuation which Marx describes in his *Robinsonia, cf. Das Kapital*, p. 43.

[1] *Dal terzo volume del ' Capitale,'* pp. 42–55.

ately owned capital and more or less free universal competition, *i.e.* in the society which produces almost exclusively *commodities*.[1]

Marx, then, in postulating as *typical* the equivalence between value and labour and in applying it to capitalist society, was, as it were, making a comparison between capitalist society and a part of itself, isolated and raised up to an independent existence : *i.e.* a comparison between capitalist society and economic society as such (but only in so far as it is a working society). In other words, he was studying the social problem of labour and was showing by the test implicitly established by him, *the special way in which this problem is solved in capitalist society.* This is the justification, no longer *formal* but *real*, of his method.

It was in virtue of this method, and by the light thrown by the type which he postulated, that Marx was able to discover and define the social origin of *profit*, *i.e.* of *surplus value*. Surplus value in pure economics is a meaningless word, as is evident from the term itself ; since a *surplus value* is an *extra value*, and thus falls outside the sphere

---

[1] Hence also Marx in §4 of Chap. I. : *Der Fetischcharakter der Waare und sein Geheimniss* (I. pp. 37–50) gave a brief outline of the other economic systems of mediæval society, and of the domestic system : ' Aller Mysticismus der Waarenwelt, all der Zauber und Spuk, welcher Arbeitsprodukte auf grundlage der Waarenproduktion umnebelt, verschwindet daher sofort, sobal wir zu anderen Producktions formen flüchten (p. 42). The relation between value and labour appears more clearly in the less complex economic systems, because less opposed and obscured by other facts.

of pure economics. But it rightly has meaning and is no absurdity, as a *concept of difference*, in comparing one economic society with another, one fact with another, or two hypotheses with one another.

It is also in virtue of the same premise that he was able to arrive at the proposition : that the products of labour in a capitalist society do not sell, unless by exception, for their value, but usually for more or less, and sometimes with great deviations from their value ; which is to say, to put it shortly, *value* does not coincide with *price*. Suppose, by hypothesis the organisation of production were suddenly changed from a capitalist to a communistic system, we should see at once, not only that alteration in the fortunes of men which appeals so much to popular imagination, but also a more remarkable change : a change in the fortunes of things. A scale of valuation of goods would then fashion itself, very different for the most part, from that which now exists. The way in which Marx proves this proposition, by an analysis of the different components of the capital employed in different industries, *i.e.* of the proportion of fixed capital (machines, etc.) and of floating capital (wages), need not be explained here in detail.

And, in the same way, *i.e.* by proving that fixed capital increases continually in comparison with floating capital, Marx tries to establish another law of capitalist society, the law of the *tendency of the rate of profits to fall*. Technical improvement, which in an abstract economic society would show itself in the decreased labour required to produce the same wealth, shows itself in capitalist society in a gradual decline in the rate of profits.[1] But this section of Volume III of *Das Kapital* is one of the least developed in this little worked-out posthumous book ; and it seems to me to be worth a special critical essay, which I hope to write at another time, not wishing to treat the subject here incidentally.[2]

II

MARX'S PROBLEM AND PURE ECONOMICS
(GENERAL ECONOMIC SCIENCE)

Marxian economics not general economic science and labour-value not a general concept of value : Engel's rejection of general economic law : abstract concepts used by Marx are concepts of pure economics : relation of economic psychology to pure economics : pure economics does not destroy history or progress.

MARXIAN economics is thus a study of abstract working society showing the variations which this undergoes in the different social economic organi-

[1] *Das Kapital*, Book III., sec. III., Chaps. XIII., XIV., XV., *Gesetz des tendentiellen Falls der Profitrate* (vol. iii., Part 1, pp. 191–249).

[2] The task of Marx's followers ought to be to free his thought from the literary form which he adopts, to study again the questions which he propounds, and to work them out with new and more accurate statements, and with fresh historical illustrations. In this alone can scientific progress consist. The *expositions* made hitherto of Marx's system, are merely *materials*; and some (like Aveling's) consist entirely in a series of little summaries, which follow the original chapter by chapter and prove even more obscure. For the law of the fall in the rate of profits, see below, chap. V.

sations. This investigation Marx carried out only in reference to one of these organisations, *i.e.* the capitalist ; contenting himself with mere hints in regard to the slave and serf organisations, primitive communism, the domestic system and to savage conditions.[1]

In this sense he and Engels declared that economics (the economics studied by them), was an historical science.[2] But here, too, their definition has been less happy than the investigation itself ; we know that Marx's researches are not historical, but hypothetical and abstract, *i.e.* theoretical.[3] They might better be called researches into *sociological economics*, if the word *sociological* were not one which is employed most variously and arbitrarily.

[1] 'To follow out completely this criticism of bourgeois economics a knowledge of the capitalist form of production, exchange and distribution is not alone adequate. We ought similarly to study at least in their essential features and taken as terms of comparison, the other forms which have preceded it in time, or exist alongside of it in less developed countries. Such an investigation and comparison has hitherto been briefly expounded only by Marx ; and we owe almost entirely to his researches what we know about pre-bourgeois theoretical economics.' (Engels, *Antidühring*, p. 154). This was written by Engels twenty years ago ; and since then the literature of economic history has grown remarkably, but historical research has been seldom accompanied by theoretical research.

[2] 'Political economy is essentially an historical science.' (Engels, *l.c.*, p. 150).

[3] What is strange is that Engels (in the passage quoted in the penultimate note) says himself most truly that Marx has written *theoretical economics*, nevertheless in the sentence quoted in the last note (which appears in the same book and on the same page) he states definitely that economics in the Marxian sense is nothing but an *historical science*.

If Marx's investigation is thus limited, if the law of value postulated by him is the special law of an abstract working society, which only partially takes effect in economic society as given in history, and in other hypothetical or possible economic societies, the following results seem to follow evidently and readily : (1) That Marxian economics *is not general economic science* ; (2) that labour-value *is not a general concept of value*. Alongside, then, of the Marxian investigation, there can, or rather must, exist and flourish a general economic science, which may determine a concept of value, deducing it from quite different and more comprehensive principles than the special ones of Marx. And, if the pure economists, confined to their own special province, have been wrong to show an ungenerous intellectual dislike for Marx's investigations, his followers, in their turn, have been wrong to regard ungratefully a branch of research which was alien to them, calling it now useless, and now frankly absurd.

Such is, in effect, my opinion, and I freely acknowledge that I have never been able to discover other antithesis or enmity between these two branches of research except the purely accidental one of the mutual antipathy to and mental ignorance of each other, of two groups of students. Some have resorted to a political explanation ; but, with no wish to deny that political prepossessions are often the causes of theoretical errors, I do not consider an explanation as adequate and appropriate, which resolves itself into accusing a large number of students of allowing themselves blindly and foolishly to be overcome by passions alien to science ; or, what is worse, of knowingly falsifying their thought and constructing a whole economic system from motives of practical opportunism.

Indeed Marx himself had not the time or means to adopt an attitude, so to speak, towards the *purists*, or the *hedonists*, or the *utilitarians*, or the *deductive* or *Austrian* school, or whatever else they may call themselves. But he had the greatest contempt for the *oeconomia vulgaris*, under which term he was wont to include also the researches of general economics, which explain what needs no explanation and is intuitively evident, and leave unexplained what is more difficult and of genuine interest. Nor has Engels discussed the subject ; but an indication of his opinion may be found in his attack on Dühring. Dühring was struggling to find a general law of value, which should govern all possible types of economic organisation ; and Engels refuted him : 'Anyone who wishes to bring under the same law the political economy of Terra del Fuoco and that of modern England, can produce nothing but the vulgarest commonplaces.' He scorns the truth of ultimate instance, the eternal laws of value, the tautologous and empty axioms which Herr Dühring would have produced by his method.[1] Fixed and eternal laws are non-existent : there is then no possibility of constructing a general

[1] *Antidühring*, pp. 150, 155.

science of economics, valid for all times and in all places. If Engels had meant to refer to those who affirm the eternity and inevitability of the laws characteristic of capitalist society, he would have been justified ; and would have been aiming his blows at a prejudice which history alone suffices to refute, by showing as it does, how capitalism has appeared at different times, replacing other types of economic organisation, and has also disappeared, replaced by other types. But in Dühring's case the criticism was much beside the mark ; since Dühring did not indeed mean to set up the laws of capitalist society as fixed and eternal ; but to determine *a general concept of value*, which is quite another matter : or, in other words, to show how, *from a purely economic point of view*, capitalist society is explained by the same general concepts as explain the other types of organisation. No effort, not even that of Engels, will suffice to stop such a problem from being stated and solved ; unless it were possible to destroy the human intellect, which, in addition to particular facts, recognises universal concepts.

It would be instructive to examine the references which there are in Marx's *Das Kapital* to unfinished analyses, extraneous to his special method ; for in this dependence on analysis the researches of pure economics have their origin. What is, for instance, *abstract human labour* (*abstrakt menschliche Arbeit*) a concept which Marx uses like a postulate ? By what *method* is that reduction of *complex* to *simple* labour accomplished, to which he refers as to an obvious and ordinary matter ? And if, in Marx's hypothesis, *commodities* appear as *congealed labour*, or *crystalised labour*, why by another hypothesis, should not all economic goods and not only commodities, appear as *congealed methods of satisfying needs* or as *crystalised needs* ? I read at one point in *Das Kapital* : 'Things which in themselves are not commodities, *e.g.* knowledge, honour, etc., may be sold by their owners ; and thus, by means of their price, acquire the form of commodities. A thing may formally have a price without having a value. The expression of the price here becomes *imaginary* like certain quantities in mathematics.'[1] Here is yet another difficulty, indicated but not overcome. Where are these *formal* or *imaginary* prices to be found ? And what are they ? By what laws are they governed ? Or are they perhaps like the Greek words in Latin prosody, which according to the school rule, *per Ausoniae fines sine lege vagantur*?—Questions of this kind are answered by the researches of pure economics.

The philosopher Lange also, who rejected Marx's law of value, which he regarded as an *extravagant production, a child of sorrow*, thinking it unsuitable—and in this he was justified, as a general law of value, arrived at the solutions which have since been given of the latter, a long time before the researches of the purists came into blossom. 'Some years ago,' he wrote in his book

[1] *Das Kapital*, I, p. 67.

on labour problems, ' I too worked at a new theory of value, *which should be of such a character as to show the most extreme cases of variation in value as special cases of the same formula.*' And, whilst adding that he had not completed it, he intimated that the course which he attempted was the same as that hastily glanced at by Jevons in his *Theory of political economy*, published in 1871.[1]

To any of the more cautious and moderate Marxians it is plainly evident that the researches of the Hedonists are not merely to be rejected as erroneous or unfounded ; and hence an attempt has been made to vindicate them in reference to the Marxian doctrine as an *economic psychology*, having its place alongside of true economics itself. But this definition contains a curious equivocation. Pure economics is quite apart from psychology. Indeed, to begin with, it is hard to fix the meaning of the words *economic psychology*. The science of psychology is divided into *formal and descriptive*. In formal psychology there is no place either for economic fact nor for any other fact which may represent a particular content. In descriptive psychology, it is true, are included representations, sentiments and desires of an economic content, but included as they appear in reality, mixed with the other psychical phenomena of different content, and

---

[1] F. A. LANGE, *Die Arbeiterfrage*, 5th ed., Winterthur, 1894, (the author's last revision was in 1874) see p. 332 ; *cf.* p. 248 and on p. 124, the quotation from Gossen's book, then very little known.

inseparable from them. Thus *descriptive economic psychology* can be, at most, an approximate limitation, by which we take as a subject of special description the way in which men (at a given time and place, or even in the mass as hitherto they have appeared in history) think, feel and desire in respect to a certain class of goods which are usually called material or economic, and which, however, stand in need of specification and definition. Subject-matter, in truth, better suited to history than to science, which regards such matters only as empty and unimportant generalisations. This may be seen in the long discussion of the matter by that most weighty of pedants, Wagner, in his manual, which, of all that has been written on the question, I think the most worthy of notice, and which is yet, in itself, a thing very little worthy of notice or conclusive.[1] An enumeration and description of the various tendencies which exist in men as they appear in ordinary life : egoistical and altruistic tendencies, love of self-advantage and fear of disadvantage, fear of punishment and hope of reward, sense of honour and fear of disgrace and public contempt, love of activity and dislike of idleness, feeling of reverence for the moral code, etc., this is what Wagner calls *economic psychology* ; and which might better be called: *various observations in descriptive psychology, to be*

[1] ADOLF WAGNER, *Grundlegung der politischen œkonomie*, 3rd Ed., Leipzig, 1892, vol. I, pt. I ; Bk. I, ch. i. *Die Wirthschaftliche Natur des Menschen*, pp. 70-137.

kept in mind whilst studying the practical questions of economics.[1]

But what, pray, has pure economics in common with psychology? The purists start from the hedonistic postulate, *i.e.* from the economic nature itself of man, and deduce from it the concepts of *utility* (*economic* utility which Pareto has proposed to call by a special name, *ofelimita*, from the Greek ὠφέλιμος) of *value*, and directly, all the other special laws in accordance with which man behaves in so far as he is an abstract *homo oeconomicus*. They do exactly what the science of ethics does with the moral nature ; and the science of logic with the logical nature ; and so on. At this rate then would ethics be a *psychology of ethics* and logic a *psychology*

---

[1] I may be allowed to remark that in similar discussions, economists usually make the serious mistake *of making the concept economic coincide with the concept egoistic.* But the economic is an independent sphere of human activity, in addition to all the others, such as the spheres of ethics, æsthetics, logic, etc. The moral *goods* and the satisfaction of the higher moral *needs* of man, just because they are *goods*, and *needs*, are taken into account in economics, but still *only as goods and needs*, not as *moral* or *immoral, egoistic* or *altruistic.* In like manner, a *manifestation* (by words or by any other means of expression) is taken into account in æsthetics ; but only *as a manifestation* not *as true, false, moral, immoral, useful, harmful, etc.* Economists are still impressed by the fact that Adam Smith wrote one book of theory and of ethics, and another of economic theory ; which may interpret to mean that one dealt with a theory of *altruistic* facts and the other with one of *egoistic* facts. But if this had been so, Adam Smith would have discussed, in both of his chief works, facts of an ethical character, estimable or reprehensible ; and would not have been an economist at all ; a ridiculous conclusion which is a *reductio ad absurdum* of the identification of economic action with egoism.

of logic ? And, since all that we know passes through the human mind, ontology would be a *psychology of existence*, mathematics a *psychology of mathematics*, and we should thus have confused the most diverse things, ending in a disorder the aim of which would be no longer comprehensible. Hence we conclude, that with care and the exercise of a little thought, it will necessarily be agreed that pure economics is not a psychology, but is the true and essential *general science of economic facts*.

Professor Labriola, too, shows a certain ill-humour which does not seem to me entirely justified, towards the pure economists, 'who', he says, 'translate into *psychological conceptualism* the influence of *risk* and other analogous considerations of ordinary commercial practice ! And they do well—I answer—because the mind desires to give an account even of the influences of risk and of commercial practice, and to explain their mechanism and character. And then, *psychological conceptualism* ; is not this an unfortunate connection between what your intellect shows you that pure economics really is (science which takes as its starting point an irreducible concept), and that hazardous definition of *psychology* which has been criticised above ? Are not the noun and adjective in opposition to one another ? And further, Labriola speaks contemptuously of the ' *abstract atomism* ' of the hedonists, in which, 'one no longer knows what history is, and progress is reduced to mere appearance.' [1] Here

[1] *Discorrendo di socialismo e di filesophia*, l. vi.

too, it does not seem to me that his contempt is justified ; for Labriola is well aware that in all abstract sciences, concrete and individual things disappear and that their *elements* alone remain as objects to be considered : hence this cannot be made a ground for special complaint against economic science. But *history* and *progress*, even if they are alien to the study of abstract economics, do not therefore cease to exist and to form the subject of other studies of the human mind ; and this is what matters.

For my part I hold firmly to the economic notion of the hedonistic guide, to utility-ophelimity, to final utility, and even to the explanation (economic) of interest on capital as arising from the different degrees of utility possessed by present and future goods. But this does not satisfy the desire for a *sociological*, so to speak, elucidation of interest on capital ; and this elucidation, with others of the same kind, can only be obtained from the comparative considerations put before us by Marx.[1]

---

[1] It is strange how among the students of pure economics also this need for a different treatment makes itself felt, leading them to contradictory statements and to insuperable perplexities. PANTALEONI, *Principî di economia pura*, Florence, Barbera, 1889, p. 3, Ch. iii § 3 (pp. 299-302), contradicts Böhm-Bawerk, inquiring whence the borrower of capital at interest is able to find the wherewithal to pay the interest. PARETO, *Introd. critica agli Estratti del Capitale del Marx*, Ital. trans. Palermo, Sandron, 1894, p. xxx, n. : 'The phenomena of *surplus value* contradicts Marx's theory which determines values solely by labour. *But, on the other hand, there is an expropriation of the kind which Marx condemns.* It is not at all proved that this expropriation helps to secure the hedonistic maximum. *But it is a*

III

CONCERNING THE LIMITATION OF THE MATERIAL-ISTIC THEORY OF HISTORY

Historical materialism a canon of historical interpretation : Canon does not imply anticipation of results : Question as to how Marx and Engels understood it : Difficulty of ascertaining correctly and method of doing so : How Marxians understand it : Their metaphysical tendency : Instances of confusion of concepts in their writings : Historical materialism has not a special philosophy immanent within it.

HISTORICAL materialism if it is to express something critically acceptable, can, as I have had occasion to state elsewhere,[1] be neither a new *a priori* notion of the philosophy of history, nor a new method of historical thought ; it must be simply a *canon* of historical interpretation. This canon recommends that attention be directed to the so-called economic basis of society, in order that the forms and mutations of the latter may be better understood.

The concept canon ought not to raise difficulty, especially when it is remembered that *it implies no anticipation of results*, but only an aid in seeking

difficult problem how to avoid this expropriation.' A learned and accurate Italian work which attempts to reconcile the opinions of the hedonistic school with those of the followers of Ricardo and Marx, is the memorandum of Prof. G. RICCA SALERMO, *La theoria del valore nella storia delle dottrine e dei fatti economici,* Rome 1894. (extr. from the *Memorie dei Lincei,* s. v. vol. i., pt. i.)

[1] See above, chap. I.

for them ; and is entirely of empirical origin. When the critic of the text of Dante's *Comedia* uses Witte's well-known canon, which runs : ' *the difficult reading is to be preferred to the easy one,*' he is quite aware that he possesses a mere instrument, which may be useful to him in many cases, useless in others, and whose correct and advantageous employment depends entirely on his caution. In like manner and with like meaning it must be said that historical materialism is a mere *canon* ; although it be in truth a canon *most rich in suggestion.*

But was it in this way that Marx and Engels understood it ? and is it in this way that Marx's followers usually understand it ?

Let us begin with the first question. Truly a difficult one, and offering a multiplicity of difficulties. The first of these arises so to speak, from the *nature of the sources.* The doctrine of historical materialism is not embodied in a classical and definite book by those authors, with whom it is as it were identified ; so that, to discuss that book and to discuss the doctrine might seem all one thing. On the contrary it is scattered through a series of writings, composed in the course of half a century, at long intervals, where only the most casual mention is made of it, and where it is sometimes merely understood or implied. Anyone who desired to reconcile all the forms with which Marx's and Engels have endowed it, would stumble upon contradictory expressions, which would make it impossible for the careful and methodical interpreter to decide what, on the whole, historical materialism meant for them.

Another difficulty arises in regard to the weight to be attached to their expressions. I do not think that there has yet been a study of what might be called Marx's *forma mentis* ; with which Engels had something in common, partly owing to congeniality, partly owing to imitation or influence. Marx, as has been already remarked, had a kind of abhorrence for researches of purely scholastic interest. Eager for knowledge of *things* (I say, of concrete and individual things) he attached little weight to discussions of *concepts* and the *forms of concepts* ; this sometimes degenerated into an exaggeration in his own concepts. Thus we find in him a curious opposition between statements which, interpreted strictly, are erroneous ; and yet appear to us, and indeed are, loaded and pregnant with truth. Marx was addicted, in short, to a kind of *concrete logic*.[1] Is it best then to interpret his expressions literally, running the risk of giving them a meaning different from what they actually bore in the writer's inmost thoughts ? Or is it best to interpret them broadly, running the opposite risk of giving them a meaning, theoretically perhaps more acceptable, but historically less true ?

[1] The over-abused Dühring was not mistaken when he remarked that in Marx's works expressions occur frequently 'which appear to be universal without being actually so' (Allgemein aussehen ohne es zu sein). *Kritische Geschichte der Nationalökonomie und des Socialismus*, Berlin, 1871, p. 527.

The same difficulty certainly occurs in regard to the writings of numerous thinkers; but it is especially great in regard to those of Marx. And the interpreter must proceed with caution : he must do his work bit by bit, book by book, statement by statement, connecting indeed these various indications one with another, but taking account of differences of time, of actual circumstances, of fleeting impressions, of mental and literary habits ; and he must submit to acknowledge ambiguities and incompleteness where either exists, resisting the temptation to confirm and complete by his own judgment. It may be allowed for instance, as it appears to me for various reasons, that the way in which historical materialism is stated above is the same as that in which Marx and Engels understood it in their inmost thoughts ; or at least that which they would have agreed to as correct if they had had more time available for such labours of scientific elaboration, and if criticism had reached them less tardily. And all this is of importance up to a certain point, for the interpreter and historian of ideas ; since for the history of science, Marx and Engels are neither more nor less than they appear in their books and works ; real, and not hypothetical or possible persons.[1]

[1] GENTILE, *Una critica del materialismo storico* in the *Studî storici* of Crivellucci, vol. VI, 1897, pp. 379-423, throws doubt on the interpretation offered by me of the opinions of Marx and Engels, and on the method of interpretation itself. I gladly acknowledge that in my two earlier essays I do not clearly point out where precisely the textual interpretation ends

But even for science itself, apart from the history of it, the hypothetical or possible Marx and Engels have their value. What concerns us theoretically is to understand the various possible ways of interpreting the problems proposed and the solutions thought out by Marx and Engels, and to select from the latter by criticism those which appear theoretically true and welcome. What was Marx's intellectual standpoint with reference to the Hegelian philosophy of history? In what consisted the criticism which he gave of it? Is the purport of this criticism always the same for instance in the article published in the *Deutsch-französische Jahrbücher*, for 1844, in the *Heilige*

and the really theoretical part begins; which theoretical exposition, only by conjecture and in the manner described above, can be said to agree with the inmost thoughts of Marx and Engels. In his recent book, *La filosofia di Marx*, Pisa, Spoerri, 1899 (in which the essay referred to is reprinted), Gentile remarks (p. 104), that, although it is a very convenient practice, and in some cases legitimate and necessary 'to interpret doctrines, by calling a part of their statement worthless or accidental in form and external and weak, and a part the real substance and essential and vital, it is yet necessary to justify it in some way.' He means certainly, 'justify it as historical interpretation,' since its justification as correction of theory cannot be doubtful. It seems to me that even historically the interpretation can be justified without difficulty when it is remembered that Marx *did not insist*, (as Gentile himself says) on his metaphysical notions; and did certainly insist on his historical opinions and on the political policy which he defended. Marx's personality as a sociological observer and the teacher of a social movement, certainly outweighs Marx as a metaphysician which he was almost solely as a young man. That it is worth the trouble to study Marx from all sides is not denied, and Gentile has now admirably expounded and criticised his youthful metaphysical ideas.

Familie of 1845, in the *Misère de la philosophie* of
1847, in the appendix to *Das Komnunistische
Manifest* of 1848, in the preface to the *Zur Kritik*
of 1859, and in the preface to the 2nd edition of
Das Kapital of 1873 ? Is it so again in Engels'
works in the *Antiaühring,* in the article on *Feuerbach,*
etc.? Did Marx ever really think of substituting,
as some have believed, *Matter* or material fact for
the Hegelian *Idea ?* And what connection was
there in his mind between the concepts *material* and
economic ? Again, can the explanation given by him,
of his position with regard to Hegel : ' the ideas
determined by facts and not the facts by the ideas,'
be called an inversion of Hegel's view, or is it not
rather the inversion of that of the ideologists and
doctrinaires ?[1] These are some of the questions

---

[1] I confess that I have never been able to *understand*—however
much I have considered the matter—the meaning of this
passage (which ought however to be very evident, since it is
quoted so often without any comment), in the preface to the
second edition of *Das Kapital* : 'Meine dialektische Methode
ist der Grundlage nach von der Hegel'schen nicht nur
verschieden, sondern ihr direktes Gegentheil. Für Hegel is *der
Denkprocess,* den er sogar unter dem Namen *Idee* in ein
selbständiger subjeckt verwandelt, der Demjurg des Wirklichen,
das nur seine aüssere Erscheinung bildet. Bei mir ist umgekehrt
das Ideelle nichts Andres als das im Menschenkopf umgesetzte und
ubersetzte Materielle.' (*Das Kapital* I, p. xvii.) Now it seems
to me that the *Ideelle* of the last phrase has *no relation* to the
Denkprocess and to the Hegelian *Idea* of the preceding phrase,
cf. above pp. 17. Some have thought that by the objections
there stated, I intended to deny Marx's Hegelian *inspiration.* It
is well to repeat that I merely deny the *logical relation* affirmed
between the two philosophical theories. To deny Marx's
Hegelian inspiration would be to contradict the evidence.

pertaining to the *history of ideas*, which will be answered some time or other : perhaps at present the time has not yet arrived to write the history of ideas which are still in the process of development.[1]

But, putting aside this historical curiosity, it concerns us now to work at these ideas in order to advance in theoretical knowledge. How can historical materialism justify itself scientifically ? This is the question I have proposed to myself, and to which the answer is given by the critical researches referred to at the beginning of this paragraph. Without returning to them I will give other examples, taken from the same source, that of the Marxian literature. How ought we to understand scientifically Marx's *neodialectic ?* The final opinion expressed by Engels on the subject seems to be this : the dialect is the rhythm of the development of things, *i.e.* the inner law of things in their development. This rhythm is not determined *a priori*, and by metaphysical deduction, but is rather observed and gathered *a posteriori*, and only through the repeated observations and verifications that are made of it in various fields of reality, can it be presupposed that all facts develop through negations, and negations of negations.[2] Thus the dialect would be the discovery

---

[1] Answers to several of the questions suggested above are now supplied in the book already referred to, by GENTILE : *La Filosofia di Marx.*

[2] *Antidühring*, pt. I. ch. xlii., especially pp. 138-145, which passage is translated into Italian in the appendix to the book by

of a great natural law, less empty and formal than the so-called *law of evolution* and it would have nothing in common with the old Hegelian dialect except the name, which would preserve for us an historical record of the way in which Marx arrived at it. But does this natural rhythm of development exist? This could only be stated from observation, to which indeed, Engels appealed in order to assert its existence. And what kind of a law is one which is revealed to us by observation? Can it ever be a law which governs things absolutely, or is it not one of those which are now called tendencies, or rather is it not merely a simple and limited generalisation? And this recognition of rhythm through negations of negations, it is not some rag of the old metaphysics, from which it may be well to free ourselves.[1] This is the investigation needed for the progress of science. In like manner should other statements of Marx and Engels be criticised. What for example shall we think of Engels' controversy with Dühring concerning the basis of history: whether this is

Labriola referred to above: *Discorrendo di socialismo e di filosophia,* cf. *Das Kapital,* I. p. xvii, ' Gelingt dies und spiegelt sich nun das Leben des stoffs ideell wieder, *so mag es aussehen,* als habe man es mit einer Konstruction a priori zu thun.'

[1] LANGE, indeed, in reference to Marx's *Das Kapital,* remarked that the Hegelian dialectic, ' the development by antithesis and synthesis, might almost be called an *anthropological discovery.* Only in history, as in the life of the individual, development by antithesis *certainly does not accomplish itself so easily and radically, nor with so much precision and symmetry as in speculative thought.'* (*Die Arbeiterfrage,* pp. 248-9.)

political force or *economic fact* ? Will it not seem to us that this controversy can perhaps retain any value in face of Dühring's assertion that political fact is that *which is essential historically*, but in itself has not that general importance which it is proposed to ascribe to it ? We may reflect for a moment that Engels' thesis : ' force protects (*schutzt*) but does not cause (*verursacht*) usurpation,' might be directly inverted into another that : ' force *causes* usurpation, but economic interest *protects* it,' and this by the well known principle of the interdependence and competition of the social factors.

And the class war ? In what sense is the general statement true that *history is a class war* ? I should be inclined to say that history is a class war (1) when there are classes, (2) when they have antagonistic interests, (3) when they are aware of this antagonism, which would give us, in the main, the humourous equivalence that history is a class war only when it is a class war. In fact sometimes classes have not had antagonistic interests, and very often they are not conscious of them ; of which the socialists are well aware when they endeavour, by efforts not always crowned with success (with the peasantry, for example, they have not yet succeeded), to arouse this consciousness in the modern proletariat. As to the possibility of the non-existence of classes, the socialists who prophesy this non-existence for the society of the future, must at least admit that it is not a matter intrinsically necessary to historical development, since in the future, and without classes, history, it may well be hoped will continue. In short even the particular statement that 'history is a class war,' has that limited value of a canon and of a point of view, which we have allowed in general to the materialist conception.[1]

The second of the two questions proposed at the beginning is : How do the Marxians understand historical materialism ? To me it seems undeniable that in the Marxian literature, *i.e.* the writings of the followers and interpreters of Marx, there exists in truth a *metaphysical danger* of which it is necessary to beware. Even in the writings of Professor Labriola some statements are met with which have recently led a careful and accurate critic to conclude that Labriola understands historical materialism in the genuine and original sense of a metaphysic, and that of the worst kind, a metaphysic of the contigent.[2] But although I have myself, on another occasion, pointed out those statements and formulae which seem to me doubtful in Labriola's writings, I still think, as I thought then, that they are superficial outgrowths on a system of thought essentially sound ; or to speak in a manner agreeing with the considerations developed above, that Labriola, having educated himself in Marxism, may have borrowed from it also some of its over-absolute

[1] With regard to the *abstract* classes of Marxian economics and the *real* or *historical* classes, see some remarks by SOREL in the article referred to in the *Journal des Economistes*, p. 229.

[2] G. GENTILE. *o.c.* in *Studî storici*, p. 421. *cf.* 400-401.

style, and at times a certain carelessness about the working out of concepts, which are somewhat surprising in an old Herbartian like himself,[1] but which he then corrects by observations and limitations always useful, even if slightly contradictory, because they bring us back to the ground of reality.

Labriola, moreover, has a special merit, which marks him off from the ordinary exponents and adapters of historical materialism. Although his theoretical formulae may here and there expose him to criticism, when he turns to history, *i.e.* to concrete facts, he changes his attitude, throws off as it were, the burden of theory and becomes cautious and circumspect : *he possesses, in a high degree, respect for history.* He shows unceasingly his dislike for formulae of every kind, when concerned to establish and scrutinise definite processes, nor does he forget to give the warning that there exists ' no theory, however good and excellent in itself, which will help us to a summary knowledge of every historical detail.'[2]

In his last book we may note especially a full inquiry into what could possibly be the nature of

---

[1] Labriola has indeed an exaggerated dislike for what he calls the *scholastic* : but even this exaggeration will not appear wholly unsuitable as a reaction against the method of study which usually prevails among the mere men of letters, the niggardly scholars, the empty talkers and jugglers with abstract thought, and all those who lose their sense of close connection between science and life.

[2] *Discorrendo di socialismo e di filosophia,* l. ix.

a *history of Christianity*. Labriola criticises those who
set up as an historical subject the *essence* of Christianity, of which it is unknown where or when it
has existed ; since the history of the last centuries
of the Roman Empire shows us merely the origin
and growth of what constituted the Christian
society, or the church, a varying group of facts
amidst varied historical conditions. This critical
opinion held by Labriola seems to me perfectly
correct ; since it is not meant to deny, (what I
myself, do not deny) the justification of that method
of historical exposition, which for lack of another
phrase, I once called *histories by concepts*,[1] thus distinguishing it from the historical exposition of the life
of a given social group in a given place and during
a given period of time. He who writes the *history
of Christianity*, claims in truth, to accomplish a task
somewhat similar to the tasks of the historians of
literature, of *philosophy*, of *art* : *i.e.* to isolate a body
of facts which enter into a fixed concept, and to
arrange them in a chronological series, without
however denying or ignoring the source which
these facts have in the other facts of life, but
keeping them apart for the convenience of more detailed consideration. The worst of it is that whereas
literature, philosophy, art and so on are determined
or determinable concepts, Christianity is almost
solely a bond, which unites beliefs often intrinsically very diverse ; and, in writing the history of

[1] *In torno alla storia della cultura* (Kulturgeschichtein *Atti* dell
Accad. Pont. ; vol. xxv. 1895, p. 8.)

Christianity, there is often a danger of writing in reality the history of a *name, void without substance.*[1]

But what would Labriola say if his cautious criticism were turned against that *history of the origin of the family, of private property and of class distinctions,* which is one of the most extensive historical applications made by the followers of Marx : desired by Marx, sketched out by Engels on the lines of Morgan's investigations, carried on by others. Alas, in this matter, the aim was not merely to write, as could, perhaps, have been done, a useful manual of the historical facts which enter into these three concepts, but actually an *additional history* was produced: A history, to use Labriola's own phrase, of the *essence* family, of the *essence* class and of the *essence* private property, with a predetermined cadence. A ' history of the family,' to confine ourselves to one of the three groups of facts,—can only be an enumeration and description of the particular forms taken by the *family* amongst different races and in the course of time : a series of particular histories, which unite themselves into a general concept. It is this which is offered by Morgan's theories, expounded by Engels, which

[1] ' If by Christianity is meant merely the sum of the beliefs and expectations concerning human destiny, these beliefs'— writes Labriola—'vary as much, in truth, as in the difference, to mention only one instance, between the free will of the Catholics after the Council of Trent, and the absolute determination of Calvin !' (*L.c.* ix.)

theories modern criticism have cut away on all sides.[1] Have they not allowed themselves to presuppose, as an historical stage, through which all races are fated to pass, that chimerical matriarchate, in which the mere reckoning of descent through the mother is confused with the predominance of woman in the family and that of woman in society ? Have we not seen the reproofs and even the jeers directed by some Marxians against those cautious historians who deny that it is possible to assert, in the present condition of the criticism of sources, the existence of a primitive communism, or a matriarchate, amongst the Hellenic races ? Indeed, I do not think that throughout this investigation proof has been given of much critical foresight.

I should also like to call Labriola's attention to another confusion, very common in Marxian writings, between *economic forms of organisation* and *economic epochs*. Under the influence of evolutionist positivism, those divisions which Marx expressed in general : the *Asiatic*, the *antique*, the *feudal* and the *bourgeois* economic organisation, have become four historical *epochs* : *communism*, *slave organisation*, *serf organisation*, and *wage-earning organisation*. But the modern historian, who is indeed not such a superficial person as the ordinary Marxians are accustomed to say, thus sparing themselves the

---

[1] Without referring to the somewhat unmethodical work of Westermarck, *History of Human Marriage*, see especially Ernst Grosse's book, *Die Formen der Familie und die Formen des Wirthschaft*, Freiburg in B., 1896.

trouble of taking a share in his laborious procedure, is well aware that there are four *forms* of economic organisation, which succeed and intersect one another in actual history, often forming the oddest mixtures and sequences. He recognises an Egyptian mediævalism or feudalism, as he recognises an Hellenic mediævalism or feudalism ; he knows too of a German *neo-mediævalism* which followed the flourishing bourgeois organisation of the German cities before the Reformation and the discovery of the New World ; and he willingly compares the general economic conditions of the Greco-Roman world at its zenith with those of Europe in the sixteenth and seventeenth centuries.

Connected with this arbitrary conception of historical epochs, is the other of the inquiry into *the cause* (note carefully ; into the cause) of the transition from one form to another. Inquiry is made, for instance, into the *cause* of the abolition of slavery, which must be the *same*, whether we are considering the decline of the Greco-Roman world or modern America ; and so for serfdom, and for primitive communism and the capitalist system : amongst ourselves the famous Loria has occupied himself with these absurd investigations, the perpetual revelation of a single cause, of which he himself does not know exactly whether it be the earth, or population or something else—yet. it should not take much to convince us, (it would suffice for the purpose to read, with a little care, some books of narrative history), that the transition from one form of economic, or more generally, social, organisation, to another, is not the result of a *single cause*, nor even of *a group of causes which are always the same* ; but is due to causes and circumstances which need examination for each case since they usually vary for each case. Death is death ; but people die of many diseases.

But enough of this ; and I may be allowed to conclude this paragraph by reference to a question which Labriola also brings forward in his recent work, and which he connects with the criticism of historical materialism.

Labriola distinguishes between historical materialism as an interpretation of history, and as a general conception of life and of the universe (*Lebens-und-Weltanschauung*), and he inquires what is the nature of the *philosophy immanent* in historical materialism ; and after some remarks, he concludes that this philosophy is the *tendency to monism*, and is a *formal* tendency.

Here I take leave to point out that if into the term *historical materialism two different things* are intruded, *i.e.* : (1) a method of interpretation ; (2) a definite conception of life and of the universe ; it is natural to find a philosophy in it, and moreover with a tendency to monism, because it was included therein at the outset. What close connection is there between these two orders of thought ? Perhaps a logical connection of *mental coherence* ? For my part, I confess that I am unable to see it. I believe, on the contrary, that Labriola, this time, is simply stating *à propos* of historical materialism what he thinks to be the necessary attitude of modern thought with regard to the problems of ontology ; or what, according to him, should be the standpoint of the socialist opinion in regard to the conceptions of optimism and pessimism; and so on. I believe, in short, that he is not making an *investigation* which will reveal the philosophical conceptions underlying historical materialism ; but merely a *digression*, even if a digression of interest and importance. And how many other most noteworthy opinions and impressions and sentiments are welcomed by socialist opinion ! But why christen this assemblage of new facts by the name of historical materialism, which has hitherto expressed the well-defined meaning of a way of interpreting history ? Is it not the task of the scientist to distinguish and analyse what in empirical reality and to ordinary knowledge appears mingled into one ?

IV

OF SCIENTIFIC KNOWLEDGE IN FACE OF SOCIAL PROBLEMS

Socialism and free trade not scientific deductions : Obsolete metaphysics of old theory of free trade : Basis of modern free trade theories not strictly scientific though only possible one : The desirable is not science nor the practicable : Scientific law only applicable under certain conditions : Element of daring in all action.

IT has become a commonplace that, owing to Marx's work, socialism has passed *from utopia to science*, as the title of a popular booklet by Engels expresses it ; and *scientific socialism* is a current term. Professor Labriola does not conceal his doubts of such a term ; and he is right.

On the other hand, we hear the followers of other leaders, for instance the extreme free traders (to whom I refer by preference *honoris causa*, because they, too, are amongst the *idealists* of our times), in the name of science itself, condemn socialism as *anti-scientific* and declare that free trade is the only scientific opinion.

Would it not be convenient if both sides retraced their steps and mortified their pride a little, and acknowledged that *socialism and free trade* may certainly be called *scientific* in metaphor or hyperbole ; but that neither of them are, or ever can be, scientific deductions ? And that thus the problem of socialism, of free trade and of any other practical social programme, may be transferred to another region ; which is not that of pure science, but which nevertheless is the only one suited to them ?

Let us pause for an instant at free trade. It presents itself to us from two points of view, *i.e.* with a two-fold justification. In the older aspect it undeniably has a metaphysical basis, consisting in that conviction of the goodness of natural laws and that concept of *nature* (natural law, state of nature, etc.) which, proceeding from the philosophy of the 17th century, was predominant in the 18th century.[1] 'Do not hinder Nature in her work and all will be for the best.' A similar note is struck, only indirectly, by a criticism like that of Marx; who, when analysing the concept of *nature*, showed that it was the idealogical complement of the historical development of the middle class, a powerful weapon of which this class availed itself against the privileges and oppressions which it intended to overthrow.[2] Now this concept may indeed have originated as a weapon made occasional use of historically, and nevertheless be intrinsically true. *Natural law* in this case, is equivalent to *rational law* ; it is necessary to deny both the rationality and the excellence of this law. Now, just because of its metaphysical origin, this concept can be rejected altogether, but cannot be refuted in detail— it disappears with the metaphysic of which it was a part, and it seems at length to have really disappeared. Peace to the *sublime goodness* of natural laws.

But free trade presents itself to us, among its more recent supporters, in a very different aspect —the free traders, abandoning metaphysical postulates, assert two theses of practical importance : (*a*) that of an *economic hedonistic maximum*, which they suppose identical with the maximum of social de-

[1] This connection is shortly but carefully dealt with by IN-GRAM, *History of Political Economy*, Edinburgh, A. & C. Black, 1888, p. 62.

[2] See, amongst many passages, MARX, *Misère de la philosophie*, p. 167, *et seq.* ENGELS, *Antidühring*, p. 1, *et seq.*

sirability ;[1] and (*b*) the other, that this hedonistic maximum can only be completely secured by means of the fullest economic liberty. These two theses certainly take us outside metaphysics and into the region of reality ; but not actually into the region of science. Indeed the first of them contains a statement of the ends of social life, which may perhaps be welcome, but is not a deduction from any scientific proposition. The second thesis cannot be proved except by reference to experience, *i.e.* to what we know of human psychology, and to what, by approximate calculation, we may suppose that psychology will still probably be in the future. A calculation which can be made, and has been made with great acumen, with great erudition and with great caution and which hence may even be called scientific, but only in a metaphorical and hyperbolical sense, as we have already remarked : hence the knowledge which it affords us, can never have the value of strictly scientific knowledge.[2] Pareto, who is both one of the most intelligent and also one of the most trustworthy and sincere, of the recent exponents and supporters of free trade,[3] does not deny the limited and approximate nature of its conclusions ; which appears to him so much the more clearly

[1] On the hedonistic maxima, *cf.* Bertolini-Pantaleoni, *Cenni sul concetto di massimi edonistici individuali e collectivi* (*in Giorn, degli Econ.*, s II vol. iv.) and Coletti, in the same *Giornale*, vol. v.

[2] In regard to this metaphysical use of the word science ; there even exists in Italy a *Rivista di polizia scientifica!* And the metaphor may pass here also.

[3] *Cours d' économie politique*, Lausanne, 1896-7.

in that he uses mathematical formulae, which show at once the degree of certainty to which statements of this kind may lay claim.

And, in effect, communism (which has also had its metaphysical period, and earlier still a theological period) may, with entire justice, set against the two theses of free trade, two others of its own which consist : (*a*) in a different and not purely economic estimate of the maximum of social desirability ; (*b*) in the assertion that this maximum can be attained, not through extreme free trade, but rather through the organisation of economic forces ; which is the meaning of the famous saying concerning the *leap from the reign of necessity* (=free competition or anarchy) *into that of liberty* (=the command of man over the forces of nature even in the sphere of the social natural life). But neither can these two theses be proved ; and for the same reasons. Ideals cannot be proved ; and empirical calculations and practical convictions are not science. Pareto clearly recognises this quality in modern socialism ; and agrees that the communistic system, as a system, is perfectly conceivable, *i.e.* theoretically it offers no internal contradictions (§ 446). According to him it clashes, not with scientific laws, but with *immense practical difficulties* (*l.c.*) such as the difficulty of adopting technical improvements without the trial and selection secured by free competition ; the lack of stimuli to work ; the choice of officials, which in a communistic society would be guided, still according to him, not by wholly technical reasons, as in modern industry, but on political and social grounds (837). He admits the socialist criticism of the waste due to free competition ; but thinks this inevitable as a practical way of securing equilibrium of production. The real problem—he says—is : whether without the experiments of free competition it is possible to arrive at a knowledge of the line (the line which he calls *mn*) of the complete adaptation of production to demand, and whether the expense of making a unified (communistic) organisation of work, would not be greater than that needed to solve the equations of production by experiments (718, 867). He also acknowledged that there is something parasitical in the capitalist (Marx's *sad-faced knight*) ; but, at the same time, he maintains that the capitalist renders social services, for which we do not know how otherwise to provide.[1] If it be desired to state briefly the contrasts in the two different points of view, it may be said that human psychology is regarded by the free traders as for the most part, determined, and by the socialists, as for the most part changeable and adaptable. Now it is certain that human psychology does change and adapt itself ; but the extent and rapidity of these changes are incapable of exact determination and are left to conjecture and opinion. Can they ever become the subject of exact calculation ?

If now we pass to considerations of another kind, not of what is desirable, that is of the ends and means admired and thought good by us ; but of what

[1] *Cf.* also his criticism of Marx already referred to : p. xviii.

under present circumstances, history promises us ; *i.e.* of the objective tendencies of modern society, I really do not know with what meaning many free traders cast on socialism the reproach of being Utopian. For quite another reason socialists might cast back the same reproach upon free trade, if it were considered as it is at present, and not as it was fifty years ago when Marx composed his criticism upon it. Free Trade and its recommendations turn upon an entity which *now at least*, does not exist : *i.e.* the national or general interest of society ; since existing society is divided into antagonistic groups and recognises the interest of each of these groups, but not, or only very feebly, a general interest. Upon which does free trade reckon ? On the landed proprietors or on the industrial classes, on the workmen or on the holders of public dignities ? Socialism, on the contrary, from Marx onwards, has placed little reliance on the good sense and good intentions of men, and has declared that the social revolution must be accomplished chiefly by the effort of a class directly interested, *i.e.* the proletariat. And socialism has made such advances that history must inquire whether the experience that we have of the past justifies the supposition that a social movement, so widespread and intense, can be reabsorbed or dispersed without fully testing itself in the sphere of facts. On this matter too I gladly refer to Pareto, who acknowledges that even in that country of free traders' dreams, in England, the system is supported not owing to people's conviction of its intrinsic excellence, but because it is in the interests of certain *entrepreneurs.*[1] And he recognises, with political acumen, that since social movement takes place in the same manner as all other movements, along the line of least resistance, it is very likely that it may be necessary to pass through a socialistic state,—in order to reach a state of free competition (§ 791).

I have said that the extreme free traders, much more than the socialists, are *idealists,* or if one prefers it, *ideologists.* Hence in Italy we are witnesses of this strange phenomenon, a sort of fraternising and spiritual sympathy between socialists and free traders, in so far as both are bitter and searching critics of the same thing, which the former call the *bourgeois tyranny* and the latter *bourgeois socialism.* But in the field of practical activity the socialists (and here I no longer refer especially to Italy) undoubtedly make progress whilst the free traders have to limit themselves to the barrenness of evil-speaking and of aspirations, forming a little group of well-meaning people of select intelligence, who make audience for one another.[2] By this I mean no reproach to these sincere and thoroughly consistent free-traders : rather I sincerely admire them ; their lack of success is not their own fault.

[1] Sauf l'Angleterre, où règne le libre échange *principalement parcequ'il est favourable aux intérêts de certains entrepeneurs,* le reste des pays civilisés verse de plus en plus dans le protectionnisme (§. 964.)

[2] See the *Giornale degli economisti,* excellent in all its critical sections : and especially Pareto's *chronicles* therein.

I wish merely to remark that if ideals, as the philosopher says, have short legs, those of the free traders' ideals are indeed of the shortest.

I could continue this exemplification, bringing forward various other social programmes, such as that of state socialism, which consists in accepting the socialist ideal, but as an ultimate end perhaps never fully attainable, and extending its partial attainment over a long course of centuries ; and in relying for the effective force, not in a revolutionary class, nor simply in the views of right thinkers, but in the state, conceived as a creative power, independent of and superior to individual wills. It is certainly undeniable that the function of the state, like all social functions, owing to a complication of circumstances, amongst which are tradition, reverence, the consciousness of something which surpasses individuals, and other impressions and sentiments which are analysed by collective psychology, acquires a certain independence and develops a certain peculiar force ; but in the estimation of this force great mistakes are made, as socialist criticism has clearly shown : and, in any case, whether it be great or small, we are always faced by a calculation ; and one moreover, in the region of opinion, which region science may, in part, yet bring under its power, but which in a great degree will always be rebellious to it.

Oh the misuses which are made of this word *science* ! Once these misuses were the monopoly of metaphysics, to whose despotic nature they appeared suitable. And the strangest instances could be quoted, even from great philosophers, from Hegel, from Schopenhauer, from Rosmini, which would show how the humblest practical conclusions, made by the passions and interests of men, have often been metaphysically transformed into inferences from the Spirit, from the Divine Being, from the Nature of things, from the finality of the universe. Metaphysics hypostatised what it then triumphantly inferred. The youthful Marx wittily discovered in the Hegelianism of Bruno Bauer, the *pre-established harmony of critical analysis* (Kritische Kritik) under German *censorship*. Those who most frequently have the word in their mouths make a sort of Sibyl or Pythia of a limited intellectual function. But the *desirable* is not science, nor is the practicable.[1]

Is scientific knowledge then in fact superfluous in practical questions ? Are we to assent to this absurdity ? The attentive reader will be well aware that we are not here discussing the *utility* of science,

[1] It may be remarked that in the difficulty of distinguishing the purely scientific from the practical lies the chief cause of the dangers and poverty of the social and political sciences. And we may even smile at those scientists or their ingenious admirers, who claim to accomplish the salvation of the social and political sciences, by applying to them the methods, as they say, of the natural sciences. (An Italian astronomer, ingenuous as clever, has suggested the formation of sociological observatories which, in a few years would make sociology something like astronomy !) Alas ! the matter is not so simple ; all sociologists intend indeed to apply exact methods ; but how can this application succeed when one advances *per ignes* or over ground which moves ; *d'una e d'altra parte sì come l'onda che fugge e s'appressa* ? (From both sides like the wave which ebbs and flows.)

but the possibility of *inferring*, as some claim to do, *practical programmes from scientific prepositions* ; and it is this possibility only which is denied.

Science, in so far as it consists in knowledge of the laws governing actual facts, may be a legitimate means of simplifying problems, making it possible to distinguish in them what can be scientifically ascertained from what can only be partially known. A great number of things which are commonly disputed, may be cleared up and accurately decided by this method. To give an example, when Marx in opposition to Proudhon and his English predecessors (Bray, Gray, etc.) showed the absurdity of creating *labour bonds*, *i.e.* labour-money ; and when Engels directed similar criticisms against Dühring, and then again, perhaps with less justification, against Rodbertus[1] or when both established the close connection between the method of production and the method of distribution, they were working in the field proper to scientific demonstration, trying to prove an inconsistency between the conclusions and the premisses, *i.e.* an internal contradiction in the concepts criticised. The same may be said of the proof, carefully worked out by the free traders, of the proposition : that protection of every kind is equivalent to a destruction of wealth. And if it were possible to establish accurately that law of the tendency of the rate of profits to decline,

[1] See the preface of the German translation of *Misère de la philosophie*, 2nd ed. Stuttgart, 1892, and now also in French in the reprint of the original text of the same work (Paris, Giard et Brière, 1896.)

with which Marx meant to correct and widen the Ricardian law deduced from the continuous encroachments of the rent of land, it could be said, *under certain conditions*, that the end of the bourgeois capitalist organisation was a scientific certainty, though it would remain doubtful what could take its place.

This limitation '*under certain conditions*' is the point to be noticed. All scientific laws are abstract laws ; and there is no bridge over which to pass from the concrete to the abstract ; just because the abstract is not a reality, but a form of thought, one of our, so to speak, abreviated ways of thinking. And, although a knowledge of the laws may *light up* our perception of reality, it cannot become *this perception itself*.

Here we may agree with what Labriola justly felt, when, showing his dissatisfaction with the term *scientific socialism*, he suggested, though without giving any reasons, that that of *critical communism* might be substituted.[1]

If then from abstract laws and concepts we pass to observations of historical fact, we find, it is true, points of agreement between our ideals and real things, but at the same time we enter upon those difficult calculations and conjectures, from which it is always impossible to eliminate, as was re-

---

[1] The word *communism* is also more appropriate, since there are so many *socialisms* (democratic state, catholic, etc.). On the relation between the materialistic theory of history and socialism, see GENTILE, *op. cit., passim.*

marked above, the diversity of opinions and pro-
pensities.

In face of the future of society, in face of the
path to be pursued, we have occasion to say with
Faust—Who can say I believe ? Who can say I
do not believe ?

Not indeed that we wish to advocate or in any
way justify a vulgar scepticism. But at the same
time we need to be sensible of the relativity of our
beliefs, and to come to a determination in practice
where indetermination is an error. This is the
point ; and herein lie all the troubles of men of
thought ; and hence arises their practical impotence,
which art has depicted in Hamlet. Neither shall we
wish, in truth, to imitate that magistrate, famous
for miles around the district where he officiated for
the justice of his decisions, of whom Rabelais tells
us, that he used the very simple method, when
about to make up his mind, of offering a prayer
to God and settling his decision by a game of odd
and even.[1] But we must strive to attain personal
conviction, and then bear always in mind that great
characters in history have had the courage to *dare*.
' *Alea jacta est*,' said Cæsar ; ' *Gott helfe mir, amen* ! '
said Luther. The brave deeds of history would
not be brave if they had been accompanied by
a clear foresight of the consequences, as in
the case of the prophets and those inspired by
God.

Fortunately, logic is not life, and man is not

[1] *Pantagruel*, III, 39-43.

intellect alone. And, whilst those same men whose critical faculty is warped, are the men of imagination and passion, in the life of society the intellect plays a very small part, and with a little exaggeration it may even be said that things go their way independent of our actions. Let us leave them to their romances, let them preach, I will not say in the market places where they would not be believed, but in the university lecture rooms, or the halls of congresses and conferences—the doctrine that science (*i.e.* their science) is the ruling queen of life. And we will content ourselves by repeating with Labriola that 'History is the true mistress of all us men, and we are as it were *vitalised* by History.'

V

OF ETHICAL JUDGMENT IN FACE OF SOCIAL PROBLEMS

Meaning of Marx's phrase the ' impotence of morality' and his remark that morality condemns what has been condemned by history : Profundity of Marx's philosophy immaterial : Kant's position not surpassed.

LABRIOLA, with his usual piquancy, lashes those who reduce history to a *case of conscience* or to an *error in bookkeeping.*

With this he recalls us to the two-fold consideration (1) that for Marx the social question was not a moral question, and (2) that the analysis made by Marx of capitalism amounts to a proof of the laws

which govern a given society, and not indeed to a
proof of *theft*, as some have understood it,
as though it would suffice to restore to the workman the amount of his wrongfully exacted surplus
labour, so that the accounts may turn out in order,
and the social question be satisfactorily solved.[1]

Leaving the second consideration, which yet
gives us an instance of the ludicrous travesties which
may be made of a scientific theory, let us pause
for a moment over the first formula, which usually
gives the greatest offence to non-socialists ; so
much so that many of them wish to put a little
salt in the broth and complete socialism by morality.

In actual fact, offence and moral indignation
have never been caused less appropriately.

Those remarks in Marx's writings which savour
of moral indifference, bear a very limited and
trivial meaning. Consider a moment, as indeed
has been considered many times, that no social
order of any kind can exist without a basis of
slavery, or serfdom, or hired service ; that is to
say that slavery, or serfdom, or hired service are
natural conditions of social order, and that without
them a thing cannot exist, which is so necessary to

---

[1] The absurdity of this interpretation will come out clearly
if it is merely remembered that there are many cases in which
the capitalist manufacturer pays for the labour of his workman,
a price higher than what he then realises on the market : cases, it is
true, where the capitalist is proceeding towards ruin and bank-
ruptcy ; but which he cannot, on this account, always avoid.
' Marx part des recherches faites par cette école Anglaise, dont
il avait fait une étude approfondie ; et il veut *expliquer le profit
sans admettre aucun brigandage*.' (SOREL, *art. cit.*, p. 227.)

man that, at least since he was man, he has never done without it, viz., society. Faced by such a fact, what meaning would our moral judgment have, directed against these governing human beings who call themselves slave owners, feudal lords and bourgeois capitalists, and in favour of these governed human beings who call themselves slaves, serfs, free labourers; neither of whom could be different from what they are, nor could otherwise fulfil the function assigned to them by the very nature of things.[1] Our condemnation would be a condemnation of the inevitable; a Leopardian curse directed against the *brutal power which rules in secret to the general harm*. But moral praise or blame has reference always to an act of will, good or bad; and such judgments would on the contrary be directed against a fact, which has not been willed by anyone, but is endured by every one because it cannot be different. You, indeed, may lament it; but by lamenting it, you not only do not destroy it, you do not even touch it, *i.e.*, you waste your time.

This is what Marx calls the impotence of morality, which is as much as to say that it is useless to propound questions which no effort can answer and which are therefore absurd.

But when, on the other hand, these conditions of subjection are not conceived as necessary for the social order in general, but only as necessary for a

[1] See in *Antidühring*, p. 303, the historical justification of class divisions.

stage in its history ; and when new conditions make their appearance which render it possible to destroy them (as was the case in the industrial advance toward serfdom, and as the socialists reckon will happen in the final phase of modern civilisation in regard to wage earners and capitalism) ; then moral condemnation is justified, and, up to a certain point, is also effective in quickening the process of destruction and in sweeping away the last remnants of the past.

This is the meaning of Marx's other saying : that morality condemns what has already been condemned by history.[1]

I cannot manage to see any difficulty in agreeing to remarks of this kind, even from the standpoint of the strictest ethical theories. There is here no question of misunderstanding the nature of morality, and of wishing to make it into something fortuitous or relative ; but simply of determining the conditions of human progress, turning the attention from the inevitable effects to the fundamental causes, and seeking remedies in the nature of things and not in our caprices and pious wishes. It must needs be thought that the opposition proceeds, not from intellectual error, but rather from human pride, or vanity it may be, owing to which many desire to retain for their wretched words a little of

[1] From among the many passages which support this interpretation, cf. Antidühring, pp. 152-3, 206 and especially pp. 61-2, and the preface to the German translation of Misère de la Philosophie, 2nd ed. Stuttgart, 1892 pp. ix-x, cf. also Labriola, o.c. Lett. VIII.

the virtue of the divine word, which created light by its decree.[1]

[1] See LABRIOLA, *o.c. l. cit.*, the remarks on the difficulty with which the theory of historical materialism meets owing to mental dispositions, and amongst those who wish *to moralise socialism*.

One instance, in some respects analogous to this which arises from the discussions on Marx's ethics, is the traditional criticism of Machiavelli's ethics : which was refuted by De Sanctis (in the remarkable chapter devoted to Machiavelli, in his *Storia della letteratura*), but which continually recurs and is inserted even in Professor Villari's book, who finds this defect in Machiavelli : that he did not consider the *moral question*.

I have always asked myself for what reason, by what obligation, by what agreement, Machiavelli was bound to discuss all kinds of questions, even those for which he had neither preparation nor sympathy. Can it be said, by way of example, to some one who is researching in chemistry :—Your weak and erroneous spot is that you have not gone back from your detailed investigations to the general metaphysical enquiries into the principles of reality ?—Machiavelli starts from the establishment of a fact : the condition of war in which society found itself ; and gives rules suited to this state of affairs. Why should he, who was not cut out for a moral philosopher, discuss the ethics of war ? He goes straight to practical conclusions. Men are wicked—he says—and to the wicked it is needful to behave wickedly. You will deceive him who would certainly deceive you. You will do violence to him who would do violence to you. These maxims are neither moral nor immoral, neither beneficial nor harmful ; they become one of the two according to the subjective aims and the objective effects of the action, *i.e.* according to the *intentions* and the *results*. What is evident is that a morality which desired to introduce into war the maxims of peace would be a morality for lambs fit for the slaughter, not for men who wish to repel injustice and to maintain their rights. 'And if men were all good, this precept would not be good, etc., etc.' says Machiavelli himself. (*Principe*, ch. XVIII). Villari is also troubled by the old formula concerning the ' end which justifies the means' and the ' moral end ' and the 'immoral means'. It is however sufficient to consider that the *means*, just because they are *means*, cannot be divided into *moral* and *immoral*, but merely

The same feeling must perhaps be present as the basis of the horror which usually greets the other practical maxim of the socialists ; that the workman educates himself by the political struggle. But Labriola is fully justified in admiring in the advance of German socialism ' the truly new and imposing instance of social pedagogy; viz. that, amongst such an enormous number of men, particularly of workmen of the lower middle class, a new consciousness is developing, within which compete in equal degree, a direct sense of the economic situation, which incites to the struggle, and the socialist propaganda understood as the goal or point of arrival.' What means have the preachers of moral maxims at their disposal, to secure a result equal to this ? Who are these workmen who combine in associations, who read their newspapers, discuss the acts of their delegates and accept the decisions of their congresses, if not *men who are educating themselves morally* ?

But there is not only a question of vanity and pride in that feeling of aversion, which animates many with regard to the practical maxims of the

into *suitable* and *unsuitable*. *Immoral means*, unless as an expression in current speech, is a contradiction in terms. The qualification moral or immoral can only belong to the end. And, in the examples usually given, an analysis made with a little accuracy shows at once, that it is never a question of immoral *means* but of immoral ends. The height of the confusion is reached by those who introduce into the question the absurd distinction of *private* and *public* morality.

I may be pardoned the digression ; but, as I said, questions which are really analogous re-appear now in connection with the ethical maxims of Marxism.

socialists, and in the desire, which people also show, of undertaking in the name of morality or religion, the spiritual direction of the education of the working man ; nor shall we wish to be so ingenuous and complacent as to confine ourselves to such a partial explanation. There is more, there is, I might almost say, an *apprehension* and a *fear*. An apprehension, little justified, lest the political organisation of the proletariat may lead to a brutal and unrestrained outbreak of the masses and to I know not what kind of social ruin ; as if such outbreaks were not recorded by history in precisely those periods in which it is usual to suppose that the dominion of religion over conscience was greatest, —as in the *jacqueries* of the fourteenth century in France,and again in the *peasants' wars* in Germany,— and in which there was no organisation and political culture amongst the common people.[1] A *fear*, which is on the contrary thoroughly justified and arises from the knowledge that instinctive and blind proletariat movements are conquered by force ; whereas organisation combined with an enlightened consciousness, is not conquered or only suffers temporary reverses. Does not Mommsen remark, in reference to the slave revolts in ancient Rome ; that *states* would be very fortunate if they were in no other dangers besides those which might come

[1] And it would be to the point to draw a comparison between the peasants' rebellions, with which modern Italy has supplied us with another example in recent years, and the political struggles of the German workmen, or the economic struggles of the Trade Unions in England.

to them from the revolts of the proletariat, *which are no greater than the dangers arising from the claws of hungry bears or wolves?*

These statements concerning ethics and socialist pedagogy having been explained, someone might yet ask :—But what was the philosophical opinion of Marx and Engels in regard to morality? Were they relativists, utilitarians, hedonists, or idealists, absolutists, or what else?

I may be allowed to point out that this question is of no great importance, and is even somewhat inopportune, since neither Marx nor Engels were philosophers of ethics, nor bestowed much of their vigorous ability on such questions. It is indeed of consequence to determine that their conclusions in regard to the function of morality in social movements and to the method for the education of the proletariat, contain no contradiction of general ethical principles, even if here and there they clash with the prejudices of current pseudo-morality. Their personal opinions upon the principles of ethics did not take an elaborate scientific form in their books ; and some wit and some sarcasm are not adequate grounds upon which to base a discussion of the subject.

And I will say yet more ; in ethical matters, I have not yet succeeded in freeing myself from the prison of the Kantian Critique, and do not yet see the position taken up by Kant surpassed ; on the contrary, I see it strengthened by some of the most modern tendencies, and to me the way in which

Engels attacks Dühring with regard to the principles of morality in his well-known book, does not
in truth appear very exhaustive.[1] Here again the
procedure is repeated which we have already criticised in connection with the discussions upon the
general concept of value. Where Dühring, owing
to the exigencies of scientific abstraction, takes for
consideration the isolated individual and explicitly
states that he is dealing with an abstract illustration
(*Denkschema*), Engels remarks, wittily but errone-
ously—that the isolated man is nothing but a new
edition of the first Adam in the Garden of Eden.
It is true that in that criticism are contained many
well-directed blows ; and it might even be called
just, if it refers only to ethical conceptions in the
sense of assemblages of special rules and moral
judgments, relative to definite social situations,
which assemblages and constructions cannot claim
absolute truth for all times, and all places, precisely
because they are always made for particular times
and particular places. But apart from these special
constructions, analysis offers us the essential and
ruling principles of morality, which give opportunity for questions which may, truly, be differently answered, but which most certainly are
not taken into account by Marx and Engels.
And, in truth, even if some may be able to
write on the *theory of knowledge according to*

---

[1] See in particular P. I. ch. IX., *Moral und Recht, Ewige
Wahrheiten.*

Marx,[1] to write on the principles of ethics according to Marx seems to me a somewhat hopeless undertaking.

VI

CONCLUSION

Recapitulation : 1. Justification of Marxian economics as comparative sociological economics : 2. Historical materialism simply a canon of historical interpretation : 3. Marxian social programme not a pure science : 4. Marxism neither intrinsically moral nor antimoral.

THE preceding remarks are partly attempts at interpretation, and partly critical emendations of some of the concepts and opinions expressed by Marx and in the Marxian literature. But how many other points deserve to undergo revision ! Beginning with that *concentration of private property in a few hands*, which threatens to become something like the discredited *iron law of wages*, and ending with that strange statement in the history of philosophy that *the labour movement is the heir of German*

---

[1] See, in particular, MARX's ideas : *Ueber Feuerbach*, in 1845, in the appendix to Engels' book, *Ludwig Feuerbach und der Ausgang der Klassischen deutschen Philosophie*, 2nd ed. Stuttgart, 1895, pp. 59–62 ; and *cf.* ANDLER in *Revue de metaphysique*, 1897, LABRIOLA, *o.c. passim* and GENTILE, *l.c.*, p. 319. From this point of view (*i.e.* limiting the statement to the theory of knowledge) we might speak like Labriola of historical materialism as a philosophy of practice, *i.e.* as a particular way of conceiving and solving, or rather of over-coming, the problem of thought and of existence. The philosophy of practice has now been designedly studied by Gentile in the volume referred to.

classical philosophy. And attention could thus be given to another group of questions which we have not discussed (*e.g.* to the conception of future society) in regard to their detailed elucidation and their practical and historical applications.[1] If that *decomposition of Marxism,* which some have predicted,[2] meant a careful critical revision, it would indeed be welcome.

To sum up, in the meantime, the chief results which are suggested in the preceding remarks : they maintain.

1. In regard to economic science, the *justification* of Marxian economics, understood not as general economic science, but as comparative sociological economics, which is concerned with a problem of primary interest for historical and social life.

2. In regard to the philosophy of history, the *purification* of historical materialism from all traces of any *a priori* standpoint (whether inherited from

---

[1] Some interpretations would be merely verbal explanations. To some it will appear a very hard statement that socialism aims at abolishing the State. Yet it suffices to consider that the State, among socialists, is synonymous with difference of classes and the existence of governing classes, to understand that as in such a case we can speak of the *origin* of the State, so we can speak of its *end*; which does not mean the end of organised society (*cf. Antidühring,,* p. 302). The conception of *the way in which capitalist society will come to an end* demands no little critical working out ; on this point the thought of Marx and Engels is not without obscurities and inconsistencies (*cf. Antidühring,* pp. 287 *et seq.* and p. 297).

[2] See CH. ANDLER, *Les origines du socialisme d'état en Allemagne,* Paris, Alcan, 1897. Andler promises a book, and is now giving a course of lectures on the *decomposition of Marxism.*

Hegelianism or an infection from ordinary evolutionism) and the understanding of the theory as a simple, albeit a fruitful, *canon* of historical interpretation.

3. In regard to practical matters, the *impossibility of inferring* the Marxian social programme (or, indeed, any other social programme) from the propositions of pure science, since the appraisement of social programmes must be a matter of empirical observations and practical convictions ; in which connection the Marxian programme cannot but appear one of the noblest and boldest and also one of those which obtain most support from the objective conditions of existing society.

4. In regard to ethics, the *abandonment of the legend* of the intrinsic *immorality* or of the intrinsic *anti-ethical* character of Marxism.

I will add a remark on the second point. Many will think that if historical materialism is reduced to the limits within which we have confined it, it will not only no longer be a legitimate and real scientific theory (which we are indeed prepared to grant) but will actually lose all importance whatever, and against this second conclusion we once more, as we have done already on another occasion, make vigorous protest. Undoubtedly the horror expressed by some for pure science and for abstractions is inane, since these intellectual methods are indispensable for the very knowledge of concrete reality ; but no less inane is the complete and exclusive worship of abstract propositions, of *defini-*

tions, of *theorems,* of *corollaries* : almost as if these constituted a sort of aristocracy of human thought. Well! the economic purists (not to draw examples from other fields, though numbers could be found in pure mathematics) prove to us, in fact, that the discovery of scientific theorems,—strictly, unimpeachably scientific,—is frequently neither an overimportant nor over-difficult matter. To be convinced thereof we need only remark how many *eponimi* of new theorems issue from every corner of the German or English schools. And concrete reality, *i.e.* the very world in which we live and move, and which it concerns us somewhat to know, slips out, unseizable, from the broad-meshed net of abstractions and hypotheses. Marx, as a sociologist, has in truth not given us carefully worked out definitions of *social phenomena,* such as may be found in the books of so many contemporary sociologists, of the Germans Simmel and Stammler, or of the Frenchman Durckheim ; but he teaches us, although it is with statements approximate in content and paradoxical in form, to penetrate to what society is in its *actual truth.* Nay, from this point of view, I am surprised that no one has thought of calling him ' the most notable *successor* of the Italian Niccolo Machiavelli ' ; a Machiavelli of the labour movement.

And I will also add a remark on the third point —if the social programme of Marxism cannot be *wholly included* in Marxian science, or in any other science, no more can the daily practice of socialist politics be, in its turn, *wholly included* in the general principles of the programme, which programme, if we analyse it, determines (1) *an ultimate end*, (the technical organisation of society) ; (2) *an impulse, based on history*, towards this end, found in the objective tendencies of modern society (the necessity for the abolition of capitalism and for a communistic organisation, as the one possible *form of progress*); (3) *a method* (to accelerate the final phases of the bourgeoisie, and to educate politically the class destined to succeed them). Marx, owing to his political insight, has for many years in a striking manner, joined with, and guided by his advice and his work, the international socialist movement; but he could not give *precepts* and *dogmas* for every contingency and complication that history might produce. Now *the continuation of Marx's political work is much more difficult than the continuation of his scientific work*. And, if, in continuing the latter, the so-called Marxians have sometimes fallen into a *scientific dogmatism* little to be admired, some recent occurrences remind us of the danger, that the continuation of the former may also degenerate into a dogmatism with the worst effects, *i.e.* a *political dogmatism*. This gives food for thought to all the more cautious Marxians, amongst whom are Kautsky and Bernstein in Germany, and Sorel in France; Labriola's new book, too, contains serious warnings on the matter.

November, 1897.

CHAPTER IV. RECENT INTERPRETATIONS OF THE MARXIAN THEORY OF VALUE AND CONTROVERSIES CONCERNING THEM

I

Labriola's criticism of method and conclusions of preceeding essays answered: His criticism merely destructive ; Tendency of other thinkers to arrive at like conclusions.

I HAVE always discussed frankly the views expressed in the writings of my eminent friend Professor Antonio Labriola. I am therefore glad that he has taken the same liberty with me, and has subjected to a vigorous criticism (in the French edition of his book on *Socialismo e la filosofia*),[1] my interpretation of the Marxian theory of value.[2] Labriola has been impelled to this also from a wish to prevent my opinions from appearing, 'to the reader's eyes,' as a supplement, approved by him, of his own personal ones. And though I do not think that 'to the reader's eyes' (I will however add *intelligent* readers), this would be possible, since, I have always carefully indicated the points, and they are neither few nor unimportant, where we disagree : yet being convinced that clearness is never superfluous, I welcome his intention to make it still

[1] *Socialisme et philosophie* by ANTONIO LABRIOLA. Paris, Giard et Briere, 1899, see pp. 207-224. Postscript to the French edition.

[2] See chap. III.

plainer that I am not he, and that he thinks with his mind whilst I think with mine.

Labriola rejects entirely the method adopted by me, which he describes variously as *scholastic, metaphysical, metaphorical, abstract, formal logic*. When I take pains to point out the differences between *homo œconomicus* and man, moral or immoral, between personal interest and egoism,[1] he shrugs his shoulders, he does not refuse a certain indulgence to this *traditional scholasticism*, and compares me to the man in the street who speaks of the rising or setting of the sun, or of *shining light* and *warm heat*. When I firmly maintain the theoretical necessity for a *general economics* in addition to the heterogeneous considerations of sociological economics, he taxes me with creating, *in addition to all the visible and tangible animals, an animal as such*. And he charges me, moreover, with wishing to attack history, comparative philology and physiology in order to substitute for all these the plain *Logic* of Port Royal, so that instead of studying examples of epigenesis which have actually occurred, such as the transitions from invertebrates to vertebrates, from primitive communism to private property in land, from undifferentiated roots to the systematic differentiation of nouns and verbs in the Ariosemitic group, it might suffice to register these

---

[1] Like an impenitent sinner I shall come back to this distinction, which is essential for the solid foundation of the principles of economics, and the evil effects of whose neglect are apparent in the discourses of economists.

facts in concepts passing from the more general to the more particular, in the series A a¹ a² a³ etc.

But I hardly know how to defend myself seriously from such accusations, because it obliges me to repeat what is too obvious, *i.e.*, that to make concepts does not mean to *create entities*; that to employ metaphors (and language is all metaphor), does not mean to *believe mythology*; that to construct experiences in thought, and scientific abstractions, does not mean to substitute either one or the other for *concrete reality*; that to make use, when needful, of formal logic, does not mean to ignore *fact, growth, history*. When Marx expounds historical facts I know no way of approaching him except that of historical criticism, and when he defines concepts and formulates laws, I can only proceed to recognise the content of his concepts, and to test the correctness of his inferences and deductions. Thus I have followed this second method in studying his theory of value. If Labriola knows another and better one, let him state it. But what could this *other* one possibly be ? Real logic ? In that case let us boldly re-establish Hegel, it will be the lesser evil, at least we shall understand one another. Or a still worse alternative, what monstrous empirical-dialetic or evolutionist method may it be, which confuses together and abuses two distinct procedures, and lends itself so readily to the lovers of prophecy ? Or is it merely a question of new phraseology by which we shall go on humbly working, more or less well, with the old methods, whilst detesting the old words ? Or again, is this dislike for formal logic nothing but a convenient pretext for dispensing with any vindication of the concepts which are employed ?

Marx has stated his concept of *value* ; has expounded a process of transformation of *value* into *price* ; has reconstructed the nature of profit as *surplus value*. For me the whole problem of Marxian criticism is confined within these limits :—Is Marx's conception substantially erroneous (entirely, owing to false premises, and partially, owing to false deductions)? or, is Marx's conception substantially correct, but has it been subsumed under a category to which it does not belong, and has search been made in it for what it cannot supply, whilst what it actually offers has been ignored ? Having come to this second conclusion I have asked myself : Under what conditions and assumptions is Marx's theory *thinkable* ? And this question I have tried to answer in my essay.

What Marx wished to do, or mistakenly thought himself to be doing is, I think, of interest to criticism up to a certain point ; although the history of science shows that thinkers have not always had the clearest and plainest knowledge of the whole of their thought ; and that it is one thing to discover a truth, and another to define and classify the discovery when made. It may be allowed that he who confuses ideological with historical research thus best reproduces Marx's *spirit* ; but in this case the work will be an artistic recasting or a psychological reproduction, not a criticism ; and will gather up with the sound also the unsound portion of Marx's thought.

To go into details. Labriola tries to prove the emptiness or vagueness of some of my definitions and the falsity of some of my reasoning. I having asserted that capitalist economics is a special case of general economics, Labriola remarks, ' *en passant*,' that it is nevertheless the only case which has given rise to a theory and to divisions of schools ; and I acknowledge that I do not understand the point of this remark, although it is said to be made '*en passant*.' Both Marx and Engels lamented that the ancient and medieval economic sytems had not been studied in the same way as the modern. Thus there are conceivable at least three economic theories, ancient, medieval and modern, and is it not lawful to construct a general economics ; *i.e.* to study in isolation that common *element* which causes these three groups of facts to be all three denoted by a common name ? Labriola then asks what this general and extra-historical economics can consist of, and whether it can never be of service to the conjectural psychology of primitive man : he jests after the manner of Engels, who in truth has sometimes joked too much during a discussion on serious matters. Is it incredible that I too should jest ? But I do not think there is occasion to do so ! He wonders at my *insatiability*, because having accepted the hedonistic theories, I wish to accept Marx's theories too : as though my

entire proof was not intended to make it plain that
the antithesis between these theories exists only in
imagination ; and that Marx's theory is not an
economic system entirely opposed to other systems
('*quelque chose de tout-à-fait opposé*' are Labriola's
own words), but a special and partial inquiry ; and
as though by hedonism I meant all the personal
convictions, philosophical, historical and political,
of those who follow, or say that they follow, its
guidance, and not indeed *only what follows legiti-
mately from its axiom*. When I call the explanation
of the nature of profits, offered by the hedonistic
school, an *economic explanation*, he inquires sarcastic-
ally : 'Could it possibly be *non-economic* ?' But my
statement contains no pleonasm : the adjective
economic is added to mark off the hedonistic explanation from that of Marx, which, to my thinking, is not purely economic, but historical and
comparative, or sociological, if it is preferred. He
wonders that I speak of a *working society*, and asks :
'As opposed to what ?' 'Perhaps to the saints in
paradise ?' But I have pointed out the opposition
between a hypothetical *working society*,—*i.e.* such
that all its goods are produced by labour,—and a
society, economic certainly, but not exclusively
working, because it enjoys goods given by nature,
as well as the products of labour. The saints in
paradise form another irrelevant jest.

I called Marx's concept of *surplus-value* a *concept
of difference* ; and Labriola reproaches me for not
being able 'to say exactly what I understand by

these words.' And yet I am not in the habit of speaking or writing when I do not exactly know what I want to say ; and here I believe that I have clearly expressed a thought which I had exceedingly clearly in my mind. Let us take two types of society : type A consisting of 100 persons, who, with capital held in common and equal labour, produce goods which are divided in equal proportions ; type B consisting of 100 persons, 50 of whom own the land and the means of production, *i.e.* are capitalists, and 50 are shut out from this ownership, *i.e.* are proletarians and workmen ; in the distribution, the former receive, in proportion to the capital which they employ, a share in the products of the labour of the latter. It is evident that in type A there is no place for *surplus value*. But neither in type B are you justified in giving the name *surplus-value* to that portion of the products which is swallowed up by the capitalists, except when *you are comparing* type B with type A, and *are considering the former as a contrast to the latter*. If type B is considered by itself, which is precisely what the pure economists do and ought to do, the product which the 50 capitalists appropriate, *i.e.* their profits, is a result of mutual agreement, arising out of different comparative degrees of utility. Turn in every direction and in pure economics you will find nothing more. The expropriatory character of profit can be asserted only when to the second society, we apply, almost like a chemical reagent, the standard, which, on the other hand, is characteristic of a type of society founded on human equality, a type 'which has attained the solidity of a popular conviction'(Marx). Profit ' is surplus-labour *not paid for*,' says Marx, and it may be so ; but *not paid for* in reference to what ? In existing society it is certainly paid for, by the price which it actually secures. It is a question then, of determining in what society *it would have that price* which in existing society *is denied it*. And then, indeed, it is a question of *comparison*.

The following of Labriola's assertions is not original, but is nevertheless quite gratuitous : ' Pure economics is so little extra-historical, that it has borrowed the data from real history, of which it makes two absolute postulates : the freedom of labour and the freedom of competition, pushed to their extreme by hypothesis.' If I open Pantaleoni's well-known treatise, I read in the very first paragraph of the *Teoria del valore*, Ferrara's fundamental theory that : ' value is above all a phenomenon of the *economics of the individual or isolated person*.' So little do the legal conditions of society enter into the necessary postulates of pure economics.

After which, Labriola ought not to be horrified if I have written : ' that Marx has taken his celebrated equivalence [1] " between value and labour from

---

[1] I write *equivalence* because Marx writes thus, and because for the present question this other is quite irrelevant : viz. whether the relation of value can be expressed in the mathematical form of a relation of equivalence. But, for my part, and I follow the hedonists in this ; I deny entirely that the relation of value is a relation of equivalence. The proof of this has already been supplied by others, and there is no occasion to repeat it.

outside the field of pure economics.' He will ask me : from whence then has he taken it ? And I reply : *from a special and definite type of society*, in which the legal organisation and the pre-supposed conditions of fact make value correspond to the quantity of labour.

Labriola does not consider justified the comparison which I have drawn, (metaphor for metaphor), between the commodities which in Marxian economics are presented as the *crystallisations of labour* and the goods which in pure economics might well be called *quantities of possible satisfactions for crystallised wants.* ' Hitherto—he exclaims—only sorcerers have been able to believe, or to cause it to be believed, that by desires alone a part of ourselves might be glutinised into any goods whatsoever.' But what does *glutinise* mean ? To obtain the commodity *a* costs us *x* labour of a given kind, this is Marx's *congealed labour*. Pure economics, using a more general formula, states that it costs us that body of wants which we must leave unsatisfied : this is the form of *congealment* which pure economics might supply. There is no question, in the one case, of an objective reality, as Labriola seems to think, or in the other of an imagined sorcery ; but in both cases it is a matter of the literary use of imaginative expressions to denote mental attitudes and elaborations. In this connection Labriola, as if to limit their range, says that Marx, as an author, belonged to the seventeenth century. May I be allowed, as a humble student of literature, and the author of several investigations into the character and origin of seventeenth century style,[1] to protest. Seventeenth century style consists in ingenuity, *i.e.* in putting cold intellectuality into an æsthetic form ; hence the forced comparison, the lengthy metaphor, the play on words and the equivocations. But Marx, on the contrary, misuses poetic expressions, which give the content of his thought with unrestrained vigour. We find in him just the opposite of seventeenth century style : not a lack of connection between the form and the thought, but such a violent embrace of the former by the latter that the unlucky form sometimes runs the risk of being left suffocated.[2]

The reader will be tired of these replies to a negative criticism ; but negative criticism is nevertheless all that Labriola offers us. What is his interpretation of Marx's thought ? Or which does

[1] See CROCE *Giambattista Basile e il* ' *Cunto de li Cunti,*' Naples, 1891 ; *Ricerche ispano-italiane,* series I, last paragraph, (*Atti dell' Acc. Pontan ;* vol. xxviii, 1898) ; *I predicatori italiani del seicento e il gusto spagnuolo,* Naples, Pierro, 1899 ; *I trattatisti italiani del* ' *concettismo* ' *e Baltasar Gracian* (*Atti dell' Acc. Pontan ;* vol. xxix. 1899).

[2] LABRIOLA—who reproduces Marx's style very well here and there in his own—writes in his essay on ' *Das Kommunistische Manifest,*' 2nd Ed., p. 79. ' The *Manifesto* . . . does not shed tears over nothing. The tears of things have already risen on their feet of themselves, like a spontaneously vengeful force.' The *tears* which rise *on their feet* may make the hair rise *on the head* of a man of moderate taste ; but the expression, although violently imaginative, is not in seventeenth century style.

he accept, out of those offered ? Here Labriola is silent. It is true that on another occasion I believed that I discerned in his statement that 'labour-value is the *typical premiss* in Marx, without which all the rest would be unthinkable,' an agreement with my thesis. But I see now that I must have been deceived, and that the words must have another meaning ; which, however, warned by the unlucky attempt already made, I shall not attempt further to specify. In the meantime Sombart has *built castles in the air* ; Sorel has made *hasty* or *premature elaborations* ; the present writer *has not understood* (see p. 224). Are we then faced by a mystery ? Our friend, Labriola, relates (p. 50) a story of Hegel who is said to have declared that *one only of his pupils had understood him*. (The anecdote, I may add, is recounted by Heinrich Heine in a much wittier manner).[1] Is the same thing to be repeated with regard to Marx's theory of value ?

In truth, though without wishing to deny the difficulty of Marx's thought and of the form in which he expresses it, I think that the mystery may be at length cleared up. And I say this, not only on account of my inward conviction of the truth of my own interpretation, but also on account of the agreement in which I find myself with several critics, who, almost at the same moment, and by

---

[1] 'Als Hegel auf dem Todbette lag, sagte er :—Nur einer hat mich verstanden ! Aber gleich darauf fugte er verdriesslich hinzu. Und der hat mich auch nicht verstanden !' (*Heine. Zur Geschichte der Religion und Philosophie in Deutschland*. Bk. III).

independent methods, have arrived at results nearly similar to my own.

> ' Or, se im mostra la mia carta il vero,
> Non è lontano a discoprirsi il porto. . . .'[1]

A similar tendency shows itself in what has been written on the subject by Sombart, in 1894, by Engels in 1895, by myself in 1896, by Sorel in 1897, by myself more at length in 1897, and again by Sorel in June of last year (1898).[2] Certainly truth and falsehood cannot be decided by external signs, the intellect being the only judge of them, and a judge who allows scope for infinite appeals. But nevertheless it is natural that under the circumstances pointed out above, a feeling of hope and confidence must arise that the discussion is about to be closed, that the problem is at length *ripe for solution*.

II

Meaning of phrase crisis in Marxianism: Sorel's view of equivalence of value and labour mostly in agreement with view put forward above: An attempt to examine profits independently of theory of value: Is not possible: Surplus product same as surplus value.

I THINK it opportune, however, to return to those *elaborations* of Sorel, which Labriola summarily

---

[1] 'Now, if my map shows me true, we are not far from the sight of our haven. . . .' (Ariosto, *Orlando Furioso*.)

[2] SOMBART, in the *Archiv fur soziale Gesetzgebung und Statistik*, vol. vii., 1894, pp. 555-594 ; ENGELS in *Neue Zeit* xiv., vol. i., 4-11, 37-44 ; CROCE, *Le teorie storiche del prof. Loria* ; SOREL in the *Journal des économistes*, no. for May 15th, 1897 ; CROCE, *Per la interpretazione e la critica di alcuni concetti del marxism*, see in this volume chap. III. ; SOREL, *Nuovi contributi alla teoria marxistica del valore*, in the *Giornale degli economisti*, June 1898.

judges with such severity, in order to make some remarks about them, not in refutation but in support, and to explain a certain point where there may seem to be disagreement between us, which perhaps has no reason to exist.

But here I may be allowed to make a remark. Labriola is also waging war with Sorel : his book *Discorrendo*, etc., arising out of a series of friendly letters to Sorel, which I undertook to edit in Italy, is published in French with an appendix directed against me, and a preface directed against Sorel. The ground of the quarrel is especially in connection with the so-called *crisis in Marxism*.

Now if the *crisis in Marxism* be understood as the assertion of the need for a revision and correction of the scientific ideas, of the historical beliefs, of the material of observed facts, which are current in Marxian literature, well and good : in such a crisis I too believe. If it means also a change in the programmes and practical methods, I neither agree nor disagree, having never concerned myself with the subject in dispute. If the danger is really existent the apprehension of which seems to obsess and disturb Labriola, that a crisis in Marxism of whatever kind, or the commencement of it, may be neutralised by those to whose interest it is to lead astray and scatter the labour movement, then *provideant consules*. But whether there be crisis or no crisis, whether purely scientific or also practical, whether apprehensions are well-founded or imagined and exaggerated, all these things have no connection with the questions raised by me, which relate to the erroneousness of this or that theoretical or historical statement of Marxism, and the way in which this or that must be understood in order to be regarded as true. This is my standpoint and on this ground alone I admit discussion. I may be mistaken, but this must be proved to me. But if, on the contrary, the only answer vouchsafed to me is that the crisis in Marxism results from the international reaction, of which ingenious critics are taking advantage, I shall be left it is true, somewhat bewildered ; but I shall not on this account be convinced that the theory of value is true, in the burlesque sense, for example, in which it is expounded by Stern in his well-known propagandist booklet.

Sorel at first supposes,[1] wittily enough, that Marx had built up different economic spheres, the first of which (that of labour-value) is the simplest; the second, including the phenomenon of an average rate of profit, and the creation of cost of production, is more complex, and the third, in which is observed the effect of rent of land, is still more complex. In passing from the simple to the more complex sphere, we should find again the laws of the preceding one, modified by the new data introduced, which would have given rise to new phenomena.

In his second article he abandons this interpretation, being convinced that Marx's ideal construction

---

[1] In the article referred to, in the *Journal des Economistes*.

does not aim at supplying a complete explanation of the phenomena of economics by means of the increasing complexity of his combinations. And, in my opinion, he did well to abandon it ; not only for the excellent reason stated by him, that Marx's inquiry does not include an entire system of economics, but also because the process suggested by him does not explain why Marx, in analysing the economic phenomena of the second or third sphere, ever *used concepts whose place was only in the first one.* It does not explain what I have called the *eliptical comparison*, and herein lies the difficulty of Marx's work, or rather of the literary statement of his thought. If the correspondence between labour and value is only realized in the simplified society of the first sphere, why insist on translating the phenomena of the second *into terms of the first* ? Why give the name transformation of surplus value to what makes its appearance as the natural economic result of capital which must have (from its very nature as capital) a profit ? Does Marx offer an explanation connecting ground and consequence, or does he not rather draw a *parallel between two different phenomena*, by which the diversities illuminating the origins of society are set in relief ?

But Sorel now advances to precisely this conclusion, borrowing a happy phrase from his first article: that Marx's work is not intended to explain by means of laws analogous to physical laws, but only to throw partial and indirect light on economic reality.

The method which Marx employs in his inquiry, says Sorel, is a *metaphysical instrument* ; he makes a *metaphysics of economics*. This expression may be satisfactory or not, according to the different meanings given to the word *metaphysics* ; but the idea is accurate and true. Marx builds an ideal construction which helps him to explain the conditions of labour in capitalist society.

What are the limits of Marx's ideal construction, and in what do his hypotheses consist ? I have said that the concept of labour-value is true for an ideal society, whose only goods consist in the products of labour, and in which there are no class distinctions. Sorel does not think it necessary to eliminate as I have done, the divisions of classes. But, since he writes : ' Marx, like Ricardo, conceived a mechanical society, perfectly automatic, in which competition is always at its maximum efficiency, and exchanges are effected by means of universal information ; and he supposed that the various sociological conditions are measurable in intensity, and that the numbers resulting can be connected by mathematical formulæ ; hence in such a society, utility, demand, and commerce in commodities *are results of the divisions of classes* ; *value will not in consequence be a function of this condition*, although it is truly a function of the conditions of production ; utility, demand, can only appear in the forms of the function, *in the parameters referring to the social divisions*.' Since he, I repeat, does not in his hypothesis, make labour-value dependent on the division of classes, it seems to me that this is practically to *leave out* the fact of the division. And it is perhaps clearer to omit it explicitly.

We should have then : (1) a working economic society without differences of classes, law of labour-value ; (2) Social divisions of classes, origin of profit, which, *but only in comparison with the preceding type and in so far as the concepts of the former are carried over into the latter,* may be defined as surplus-value ; (3) Technical distinction between the different industries requiring different combinations of capital (different proportions of fixed and floating capital). Origin of the average rate of profits, which in relation to the preceding type, may be regarded as a change in, and equalisation of, surplus-values; (4) Appropriation of the land by part of a social class. Pure rent ; (5) Qualitative differences in land. Differential rent. Which rents, pure and differential, present themselves, but only in comparison with the preceding types, as cut off from the amounts of surplus-value and of profits. Sorel agrees with me that the concept of labour-value, obtained in the manner described, is not only not a law in the same sense as a physical law, but is also not a law in the ethical sense, *i.e.* one that could be understood as a rule of what ought to exist. It is a law, he says, *in an entirely Marxian sense.* This I too tried to express when I wrote in my essay : ' It is a *law* in Marx's *conception,* but not *in economic reality.* It is clear that we may conceive the divergencies in relation to a standard as the rebellion of reality in opposition to that standard, to which we have given the dignity of law.'

It seems to me that the jurist Professor Stammler in his book *Wirthschaft und Recht nach der materialistischen Geschichtsauffassung*,[1] has also made the mistake of interpreting Marx's concept as an *ideal* law. He is absolutely correct when, in rejecting Kautsky's comparison between the concept of labour-value and the law of gravity—which takes effect fully on a vacuum—whilst the resistance made by air leads to special results, he maintains that this has nothing analogous to a physical law. For him, on the other hand, Marx's law is justified (at least formally) as an attempt at investigation into what in the judgment of economists, granted the capitalist organisation of society, may be *objectively accurate*. Subjective judgments may differ, but that does not affect what ought to be an objective criterion, to divide the true from the false. But can an *objective criterion* ever be found within the sphere of economics? Anyone who has rightly understood the principle of hedonistic economics must answer no. And if Stammler brings forward such an idea, it is because in his work he expressly intends to deny the originality of economic material and the independence of economics as a science.[2]

Sorel believes that Marx's method has rendered all the assistance of which it is capable, and cannot aid the study, which it is needful to make, of

[1] See pp. 266-8, 658-9.
[2] See chap. II.

modern economic conditions. If I am not mistaken he means that the hopes of the Marxians in regard to the fruitfulness of Marx's method are futile, and that the pages which he has written in the history of economics are practically all that can be produced by it. A good part of the third volume, in which Marx shows himself a simple classical economist, and the miserable and scanty output of Marxian economic writings subsequent to Marx, would suggest that Stammler's opinion is justified by the facts.

But, whilst Sorel's book seems to me welcome in the endeavour to understand and define the score of Marx's economic inquiries, I cannot form the same judgment of another attempt made to reform the basis of Marx's system by rejecting his method, and a part of his results. I refer to a recent book by Dr Antonio Graziadei,[1] which has been much discussed during these last months. Graziadei's object is to examine profits independently of the theory of value: a course already indicated by Professor Loria, and the fallacy of which ought to be clearly evident at a glance, without its being necessary to wait for proof from the results of the attempt. A system of economics from which *value* is omitted, is like logic without the *concept*, ethics without *duty*, æsthetics without *expression*. It is economics . . . cut off from its proper sphere. But let us see for a moment how Graziadei manages the working out of his idea.

[1] *La produzione capitalistica*, Turin, Bocca, 1899.

In the first place he tries to prove that in Marx's own work the theory of profits is in itself independent of that of value. Profits he says, consist in surplus-value, *i.e.* in the difference between total labour and necessary labour. Hence it can be made to originate in surplus-value without starting from the form value itself. But he himself destroys the argument when further on (p. 10) he objects that if labour is not productive labour it does not give rise to profits. Precisely for that reason—we answer —in order to be in a position to speak of labour which is productive, Marx must start from value, and precisely for that reason, in Marx's thought, the theory of profits and the theory of value are inseparably connected.

As to the construction, on his own account, of a theory of profits which is independent of that of value, Graziadei accomplishes this in a very curious way : viz. by carefully avoiding the words *value* and *labour*, and by speaking instead only of *product*. Profits, according to him, do not arise out of surplus-labour or surplus-value, but out of surplus-product ; hence we can, and ought, in theory, to start from the concept of product and not concern ourselves with value, which is a superficial growth of the final stage of the market.

Surplus product ! But surplus-product, in so far as it is an *economic* surplus-product, is *value*. Certainly, the capitalist who pays wages in kind, and in getting back again the goods advanced by him, also appropriates the other part of the product (surplus-product), can, instead of taking this to market, consume it himself directly (as in Graziadei's hypothesis). But this does not alter the matter at all, because the fact that the product is not taken to market does not mean that it has no value in exchange : since it is true that the capitalist has obtained it by means of an exchange between himself and the labourer ; which means that he has always assessed its value in some manner.

And here we are again at the theory of value. from which we have vainly attempted to escape, Moreover, since Graziadei is essentially concerned with the economics of labour, here we are again at Marx's exact concept of labour value. *Tamen usque recurrit* ![1]

---

[1] Graziadei will allow me to point out to him that it is not the first time that he has made discoveries that turn out to be equivocal. Some years ago when carrying on a controversy, in the review *Critica sociale*, on the theory of the origin of profits in Marx's system, Graziadei (vol. IV., n. 22, 16th Nov. 1894, p. 348) wrote : 'We can very readily imagine a society, in which profits exist, not indeed with surplus-labour, but with *no labour*. If, in fact, for all *the labour* now accomplished by man was substituted the work of machines, these latter, with a relatively small quantity of commodities would produce an enormously greater quantity. Now, given a capitalist organisation of society, this technical phenomenon would afford a basis for a social phenomenon, viz. : that the ruling class being able to enjoy by itself alone the difference between the product and the consumption of the machine, would see at their disposal an excess of products over the consumption of the *labourers*, *i.e.*, a surplus-product, much larger than when the feeble muscular force of man still co-operated in production.' But here Graziadei neglects to explain how *labourers* could ever exist, and *profits* of labour, in a hypothetical society, based on *non-labour*, and in which *all the labour* actually done by man

Graziadei's book includes also some *corrections* of Marx's special theories on profits and wages. But I may be allowed to remark that the corrections to be called such ought to refer to the governing principles. New facts do not weaken a theory firmly established on fundamentals ; and it is natural that, with a change in the actual conditions, a new casuistry will arise which Marx could not discuss. Whatever forecasts he may have made in his long career as author and politician, which the event has proved fallacious—I do not believe he ever pretended :

> 'Sguaiato Giosué. . . .
> Fermare il sole.'[1]

April, 1899.

would be done by machines. What would the labourers be doing there ? The work of Sisyphus or the Danaides ? In his hypothesis the proletariat would either be maintained by the charity of the ruling class, or would end by rapidly disappearing, destroyed by starvation. For if he supposed that the machines would produce automatically a superfluity of goods for the whole of that society, then he was simply constructing by hypothesis a land of *Cocaigne*.

[1] ' As follower of Joshua . . . . to stop the sun.'

CHAPTER V. A CRITICISM OF THE MARXIAN LAW OF THE FALL IN THE RATE OF PROFITS

Interpretation here given assumes acceptance of Marx's main principles : Necessary decline in rate of profit on hypothesis of technical improvement : Two successive stages confused by Marx : More accurately a decline in amount of profit : Marx assumes that would be an increase of capital : Would be same capital and increase in rate of profits : Decline in rate of profits due to other reasons.

THIS law is set forth in the third section of the third book (posthumous) of *Das Kapital.* A few criticisms have been made of it, which vary from that of Sombart, who says that it is developed *in the most striking manner* (in glänzendster Weise), to that of Loria, who defines it as 'a metaphysical pistol shot (*sic*) from beyond the Rhine,' and thinks that he refutes it by an objection which is in fact quite inappropriate. Others have thought the law certainly true, but that it explained only partially the fact of the decline in the rate of profits and required to be combined with other laws already known to classical economics. But most of those who have studied Marx's economic theories have not examined it at all ; his opponents (like Böhm Bawerk) reject it by implication, when they reject Marx's fundamental principles ; the Marxians welcome it, German fashion, humbly and submissively, without discussion, with that lack of freedom and intellectual originality which is noticeable in all their writings.

The examination of it attempted here, rests on the same basis as Marx's theories, *i.e.* it is made from the standpoint of those who accept the essentials of these theories, and hence the premiss of *labour-value*, the distinction between *fixed* and *floating* capital, the view of profits as arising from *surplus-value*, and of the *average rate* of profits as arising from the equalisation, owing to competition, of the various rates of surplus-value. It is true that I accept all these things *in a certain sense*, which is not the sense of the ordinary Marxian, inasmuch as they are not looked upon as *laws actually working in the economic world*, but as *the results of comparative investigations into different possible forms of economic society*. But such a reservation, which relates to a question discussed by me at length elsewhere,[1] has practically no effect on the present study, whose results would be almost the same, even if these theories of Marx were interpreted in the sense which I consider erroneous. The object here is no longer to determine and define accurately Marx's fundamental concepts, but to see whether, from these concepts, even when interpreted in the current manner, it is ever possible in any way to deduce the *law of the fall in the rate of profits*. This task I think impossible.

[1] See chaps. III. and IV.

The law was derived by Marx from the study of the effects of technical improvement. Marx states that technical improvement increases the amount and changes the form of the total capital, increasing the proportion of fixed as compared with floating capital, so that by this means the rate of profit is decreased ; the latter arises, as is well-known, out of the surplus-value, the product of the floating capital divided by the total capital. He illustrates the matter thus. Some technical improvement occurs ; new machines are made, which formerly did not exist. The capital employed in production has been hitherto, we will suppose, a total of 1,000, divided into 500 fixed and 500 floating, and employing 100 labourers : the surplus-value = 500, *i.e.* the rate of it is 100 per cent ; and hence the rate of profit is $\frac{500}{1000}$ = 50 per cent. In consequence of the technical improvement, and of the construction of new machines, the 100 labourers who are maintained by the variable capital of 500, continue still to be employed in production ; but, in order that this may be possible, it is necessary to use a larger fixed capital, which we may suppose 200 larger than before. Hence, as the result of the technical improvement, there will now be a total capital of 1,200, *i.e.* 700 fixed and 500 floating ; and the rate of surplus-value remaining unchanged at 100 per cent., the rate of profit will be $\frac{500}{1200}$ = about 41 per cent., *i.e.* will have decreased from 50 per cent. to 41 per cent. Hence the necessary decline in the rate of profit on the *hypothesis* of technical

improvement. But this *hypothesis* is an actual every-
day *fact* in modern capitalist society. Hence, the
actual decline of the average rate of profits in
modern capitalist society. But this law is more or
less counteracted by other facts, which act in a contrary sense more or less transitorily. Thus the fall
is only *a tendency*.

In order that our study may be clear, it is above
all necessary to distinguish the two groups of facts,
or the two stages in the same capitalist society
which Marx confused and embraced in a single
somewhat obscure view.

The first stage is marked by the fact, pure and
simple, of a technical improvement. Now technical
improvement, among its logical, or what is the same
thing, its necessary effects, in no way includes that
of an increase in the amount of total capital employed, nor that of leaving the quantity of total
capital unchanged. It has rather exactly the opposite
as its necessary and immediate effect : *i.e.* that of
limiting the capital employed. It is unnecessary to
warn the reader that we are here treating of economic
science and that increase and decrease refer always
to *economic values*. In its simplest form, supposing
the quantity of objects produced to be constant (200
shoes are required, and there is no reason to increase
the production), technical progress will consist,
purely and simply, in a saving of social expense :
the same production at less expense. And since all
cost, in Marx's hypothesis resolves itself into social
labour, there will be the same production with less

social labour. If it were not so, it would not be worth while to introduce this technical innovation ; there would be, economically, no improvement but either the *status quo ante* or a regression. We must not take into account the other effects which would arise to increase production, greater consumption, increase of population, etc : additional and extraneous facts which are not considered here, since we are concerned with the single fact of technical improvement, all other conditions remaining unchanged. And, in such a case, we cannot represent technical improvement with the increasing series of total capital which Marx employs, viz. 150, 200, 300, 400, 500, etc., but with this decreasing one, 150, 140, 130, 120, 110, etc. And to keep to the illustration used above, if we suppose that the given technical improvement has caused a decrease of $\frac{1}{10}$ in the total social labour required, we shall have in place of the original capital of 1,000 a capital of 900, no longer made up of 500 fixed and 500 floating, but of 450 fixed and 450 floating. The decrease must affect proportionally every part of the capital since all of it is, in the final analysis, a product of labour. Of the 100 original labourers, $\frac{1}{10}$, *i.e.* 10 of them will remain unemployed : a fraction of the original capital will remain unemployed ; the quantity (or utility) of the goods produced will remain the same.[1]

[1] We here suppose a series of productive periods already rapidly passed through, which may suffice to replace the whole of the total capital by the new technical processes. It is evident how-

When the description of the facts is thus corrected, there is no doubt that the smaller total capital employed, supposing on the one hand, the rate of surplus-value to remain unchanged, and, on the other, 10 of the original labourers to be working no longer, would absorb an amount of surplus-value of 450. But the rate of profit would not on this account be changed ; or rather, just for this reason the rate of profit could not be altered and would be expressed by $\frac{450}{900}$ (as at first $\frac{500}{1000}$), *i.e.* it would be as at first, 50 per cent.

This simplest case does not then give us Marx's law, but this other law ; 'Technical improvement, supposing all the other conditions remain unchanged, causes a decrease in the *amount* (not the *rate*) of surplus-value and of profits.' this law assumes that the $\frac{1}{10}$ of the labourers left unemployed become entirely superfluous. These ten labourers are henceforth to be a dead weight supported by the charity of others, or to die of starvation, or to emigrate—to a new world. Let them be left to their fate. Social production will remain at its former level, thanks to the technical improvement, but accomplished without their help. This is the hypothesis, but given this hypothesis, of what importance is the law ? To see this clearly it will suffice

ever, that as fixed capital is replaced in successive portions, in a first stage, goods are used as capital, whose cost of *reproduction* no longer corresponds to their original cost of *production*, *i.e.* whose actual social value no longer corresponds to the original one. But to consider the separate stages would here cause a useless complication.

to push the hypothesis yet further, as we are entitled to do, and suppose that the technical improvements continuing, the employment gradually becomes superfluous, not only of $\frac{1}{10}$, but of $\frac{1}{4}$, $\frac{1}{3}$, $\frac{1}{2}$ of the labourers, *i.e.* that the employment of labourers tends to become $= 0$. In this case capitalist society as such would come entirely to an end, since the utility of labour, on which it is based, would come to an end. Where there is nothing the King loses his rights ; and where labour has no utility the capitalist loses his. The ex-capitalists would have no more workmen to impoverish, but would be changed into the owners of automatic fountains of wealth ; like those fortunate mortals in the fable enriched by charmed knives, by wonderful lamps, by gardens producing with instantaneous and spontaneous energy all God's gifts. In other words the law here resolves itself into a *truism*.

But Marx did not think of this *truism*. He wished to determine exactly the organic law of the variations in the rate of profits. In fact—as is seen in the illustration given—he does not at all suppose that the energy of labour may become superfluous ; but rather that the labourers will find fresh employment with an increase in the original fixed capital. Given technical improvement and production also will be increased ; this is the second stage which he considers. The 100 labourers are still all working, the fixed capital with which they work must be increased from 500 to 700, and the total has hence become 1200. The law which he deduces, of the fall in the rate of profits (in the illustration, from 50 per cent. to 41 per cent.) is not a *truism* ; on the contrary it presents itself with all the importance and originality of a scientific discovery. All depends on seeing whether in the scientific discovery we have indeed—the truth.

The crux of Marx's proof lies in the statement ; that the labourers who would have had to remain unemployed, find on the contrary employment, but with a capital *increased by so much* (=200) over the original. Is this statement correct ? On what does Marx base it ?

To this fundamental proposition my *criticism* refers, itself equally fundamental. If it is admitted it amounts to *a most complete denial of the truth of the Marxian law*. Nevertheless I state my idea in the form of a *criticism* and *doubtfully*, because, in dealing with a thinker of Mark's rank, it is necessary to proceed cautiously, and to remember (which I do not forget) that several times errors ascribed to him have been explained as mistakes of his opponents.

For what reason, I ask myself, do the ten unoccupied labourers, in order to be employed afresh, require a constant capital larger than the original?

The technical improvement has not diminished the natural *utility* of the production (also in our hypothesis it has not increased it either, but has left it unchanged) ; but it has only diminished its *value*. There will be then, with the improved technical organisation, raw materials, tools, clothing, foodstuffs, etc., of the same total natural utility as at first. The economic value of all these products is diminished, because in them (to employ the metaphor chosen by Marx), is congealed a smaller quantity of labour, *i.e.* less by the work of ten labourers. But from the point of view of power to satisfy wants, the raw materials, the tools, the clothing, the means of sustenance, etc., remain, in virtue of the technical improvement, of the same rank as at first. If then capitalists and workpeople have remained as temperate as before, and their standard of life has not risen (and this is in the hypothesis), the production will offer as at first means of employment and means of sustenance for the ten labourers left unoccupied. By re-employing them, *i.e.* maintaining them with the original means of subsistence, and setting them to work on the original raw materials or their new products, the capitalists will increase their production, or—what is the same thing—will improve its quality. But since we know that, economically, the value of that capital has *diminished*, it will come about that a capital *economically smaller* will absorb the same energy of labour as formerly, *i.e. the same amount of profits* ; and an equal amount of profits with a smaller total capital means an *increased rate of profits*. Exactly the opposite to what Marx thought it possible to prove.

Turning to our illustration, the ten labourers will find employment with a capital which, like the utility, has remained the same, but economically has decreased to 900. This means that the rate of profits has increased from $\frac{500}{1000}$ to $\frac{500}{900}$, *i.e.* from 50 per cent. to about 55 per cent. As to the rate of surplus-value, since the entire value of the total capital is reduced, it must no longer be calculated, as before the technical improvement, as $\frac{500}{500}$, nor as in the first stage we considered (in which the technical improvement had made a portion of the labour entirely superfluous) as $\frac{450}{450}$, but as $\frac{500}{450}$, *i.e.* it will no longer be 100 per cent., but will have risen to about 111 per cent.

To this criticism of mine I have found no answer, either explicit or implicit, in Marx's work. Only in one passage, where he speaks of the counteracting causes, and in particular of surplus population (Chap. xiv., § iv.), he hints at the case where labour power may be re-employed with a minimum capital. It may be said that here Marx passed close to the difficulty, without striking upon it, *i.e.* without becoming aware of its importance. And, if he had struck on it, I doubt whether he would have overcome it and passed on ; I think rather that his theory would have gone to pieces.

I foresee that it may be said : you have assumed that, owing to the technical improvement, not only would a number of labourers remain unemployed, but also a fraction of the original total capital, *i.e.* of means of production and means of subsistence ; and when the labourers are re-employed, it is true that during the new cycle of production, other fractions of unoccupied capital will not unite with the original fractions, but precisely for this reason the quantity of production which will result will be increased, and in the next cycle of production a still greater fraction of unoccupied capital will add itself, unless the ten labourers do not continue to be re-employed, in which case the un-occupied fraction will be smaller, but the increase will become constant. Now all these means of production and of sustenance will not be consumed (or will be partially consumed and partially saved), by the capitalist class, and hence there will be an increasing accumulation. The quantities of goods saved, owing to the impulsion of economic interest will not remain un-used in warehouses or strong boxes, but will be thrown on the market as capital seeking employment. This will increase the rate of wages, and hence will have a depressing effect on the rate of profits. Very good, but in such a case we are outside the Marxian law. The *factor* here considered, is no longer technical improvement taken by itself, but *saving*, which may be, as stated, encouraged by technical progress, but cannot be *inferred* from it. For it is true that, if we suppose the case of extravagant capitalists, saving, in spite of technical improvement will not take place. And as technical improvement encourages saving, so the latter, in its turn, by increasing wages, encourages the increase of population, and hence the reduction of wages, and once again a rise in the rate of profits. But, when saving and the increase of population come upon the scene we are already within the sphere of the law of demand and supply, *i.e.* of

ordinary, accredited economics, which Marx despised as vulgar, and out of dislike of which he
devised his law of the fall in the rate of profits
yielded by the above combination of capital owing
to the effect of technical improvement. I, indeed,
believe that only the ordinary law of demand and
supply can explain the variations in the rate of
profit : but to return to it is not indeed to defend
Marx's thesis, but rather to ratify its condemnation.

However it is regarded, this thesis seems to me
indefensible ; and even more indefensible if, leaving aside for a moment logical trains of reasoning
and arithmetical calculations, we look at it with the
clear intuition of common sense. See here—to
follow the strict hypothesis set forth by Marx—
on one side a capitalist class, and on the other a
proletarian class. What effect does technical improvement have ? It increases the wealth in the
hands of the capitalist class. Is it not intuitively
evident that, as a result of technical improvement,
the capitalists can, by anticipating commodities
whose value is continually decreasing, obtain *the same
services* which they obtained at first from the proletariat ? And that hence the relation between value
of services and value of capital will change in favour
of the former, *i.e.* that the rate of profits will increase ? When commodities (capital) are anticipat-
ed, which formerly were reproduced by five hours
of labour and now are reproduced by four, the
workman will continue to work ten hours. Former-

ly with five there were ten ; now with four there is similarly ten. The sponge costs less, but the quantity of water with which it is saturated is the same. How could Marx suppose that after technical improvement, the expenses of the capitalists would always increase, so that proportionally profits would be in a state of perpetual decline, and would end by making, in face of the total costs, a most wretched figure ?

Marx's mistake has been that he has inadvertently attributed a *greater value* to the fixed capital, which after the technical improvement is worked by the same labourers as before. Certainly anyone who looks at a society in two successive stages of technical development, will find in the second stage a greater number of machines and of tools of every kind. *This is a question of statistics, not of economics.* Capital (and Marx appears to have neglected this point for the moment) is not estimated by its physical extension, but by its economic value. And economically that capital (supposing all the other conditions remain constant) *must be worth less* ; otherwise no technical improvement would have taken place.

An external circumstance which might serve to explain Marx's error is the fact that the third book of *Das Kapital* is a posthumous work, some parts of which are hardly sketched out, and amongst these that of the *law of the rate of profits*, which, moreover, does not relate to the *establishment of principles*, but, being a consequence and an application of these, was perhaps not worked out to the same extent as the fundamental or central part of the theory.[1] It it probable that the author, if he could have gone over his rough draft again, would have materially modified it or entirely discarded it. But perhaps some internal reason could also be found for this strange mistake, in that Marx always misused the comparative method without disclosing any distinct knowledge of his procedure. And it might be that, as already in his earlier investigations, he perpetually transferred labour-value from a hypothetical society to the actual capitalist society, so in this new problem he has been led to estimate the worth of the technical capital in a more advanced society at the rate of value of that in a less advanced society. In this impossible attempt his method has here broken in his hands.

As we have disputed the actual basis of the Marxian law, it seems indeed superfluous to follow out its further developments, which are advanced in a form worked out with but little care. It is enough to remark that in these developments, as in general, throughout *Das Kapital*, there is a continuous medley of theoretical deductions and historical descriptions, of logical and of material connections. The defect, however, becomes in this instance an advantage, because many of the observations made by Marx, understood as historical

---

[1] The explanation of the way in which the average rate of profit arises belongs to the fundamental part of the third book of *Das Kapital*, and Marx must have thought it out together with the fundamental chapters in the first book.

descriptions of what usually happens in modern society, will be found to be true and can be saved from the shipwreck, as regards the theory of the law, with which by chance they are feebly connected. And it would even be possible to make such an investigation in respect to that very portion which we have disputed, *i.e.* to enquire what *facts*, actually observed by him, could have impelled Marx to construct his law, *i.e.* to give of these facts an explanation which is theoretically unjustifiable.

Marx attributed the greatest importance to the discovery of the *law of the fall in the rate of profits*. Herein lay for him ' the mystery over which all economists from Adam Smith onwards have toiled ' ; and in the different attempts to solve the problem he saw the explanation of the divergence between the various schools of economists. Ricardo's bewilderment in face of the phenomenon of the progressive decrease in the rate of profits seemed to him fresh evidence of the earnestness of mind of that writer, who discerned the vital importance of the problem for capitalist society. That the solution had not been found before his, Marx's, time, appeared to him easily explicable, when it was remembered that until then political economy had sought gropingly for the distinction between fixed and floating capital without succeeding in formulating it, and had not been able to explain surplus-value in distinction from profits, nor profit itself in its purity, independently of the separate fractions of it in competition amongst themselves ; and that, in the end, it had been unable to analyse completely the difference in the organic composition of capital, and much less, the formation of the general rate of profits.

His explanation being now rejected, a double problem presents itself. The first question relates to fact. It is needful to ask : does the fact spoken of actually exist, and how does it exist ? Has a gradual decline in the rate of profits been ascertained ? And in which countries, and in what circumstances ? The second question relates to the cause : since, whilst we have seen that there could only be one economic reason for the phenomenon, (the law of demand and supply), there may be several historical causes, and these may vary in different cases. The decline in the rate of profits may happen owing to a nominal increase in wages due to an increase in the rent of land, or it may happen owing to a real increase in wages due to stronger organisation among the workpeople, or it may happen owing to an increase, also real, in wages resulting from saving and from growing accumulations, which increase the capital in search of employment. This investigation must be made without prejudices, whether optimistic or pessimistic, apologetic or controversial ; and economists have sinned but too often in all these ways. The listeners have seized upon the result of limited and qualified investigations, now in order to sing a hymn to the spontaneous force of progress, which will gradually cause the disappearance of capitalists or reduce interest to $\frac{1}{2}$ per cent. ; now in order to terrify their audience by a spectacle no less fantastic, of landed proprietors as the sole owners of all the goods of society ![1]

May 1899.

---

[1] This is the case contemplated by Ricardo in the celebrated § 44 of chapter vi, *On Profits* : Marx appears to attach ittle importance to this case, having complete faith in the continued technical progress of agriculture, not to speak of other counteracting causes. It is necessary to add that Marx in conformity with his law, maintains that the rent of land also has a tendency to fall, although it may increase its total amount, or its proportion in reference to industrial profits : see vol. iii, 223-4.

CHAPTER VI. ON THE ECONOMIC PRINCIPLE

TWO LETTERS TO PROFESSOR V. PARETO

I

Need for more comprehensive definition of the economic principle : Reasons why the mechanical conception erroneous, economic fact capable of appraisement : Cannot be scale of values for particular action : Economic datum a fact of human activity : Distinction and connection between pleasure and choice : Economic datum a fact of will : Knowledge a necessary presupposition of will ; Distinction between technical and economic : Analogy of logic and æsthetic : Complete definition of economic datum.

Esteemed Friend,

On reading the little paper, which you were courteous enough to send me, on how to state the problem of pure economics,[1] I at once felt a desire to discuss the subject with you. Other occupations have obliged me to defer the satisfaction of this wish until now ; and this has been fortunate. The extracts from your new and still unpublished treatise on pure economics, which came out in the March number of this Review,[2] have obliged me to abandon in part the scheme of

[1] *Comment se pose le problème de l'economie pure.* Paper read in December 1898 to the *Societé Stella.*

[2] *Giornale degli economisti*, March 1900, pp. 216-235.

thought which I had in mind ; for I saw from them that you had modified some of those points in your thesis, which seemed to me most open to dispute.

I have on several occasions heard something like a feeling of distaste expressed for the endless discussions about value and the economic principle which absorb the energies of economic science. It is said that if this splitting of hairs over the scholastic accuracy of its principle were abandoned, the science might throw light on historical and practical questions which concern the welfare of human society. Apparently you have not allowed yourself to be alarmed by the threatened distaste of readers ; nor indeed am I. Can we silence the doubts which disturb us ? Could we have assurance whilst silencing these doubts that we were not endangering just those *practical* issues which the majority have at heart ? Issues which we ourselves have at heart since we are certainly not able, like the monks of old, to free ourselves from interest in *the affairs of the age*. May not science be, as Leibniz said, *quo magis speculativa, magis practica* ? We must then go our way, and endeavour to satisfy our doubts, with all the caution and self-criticism of which we are capable ; since they cannot be suppressed. On the other hand we should endeavour also not to offer our solutions to the public except when our knowledge, —wide if it may be so (yet necessarily imperfect)— of the literature on the subject, gives us some confidence that we are not repeating things already stated. Unless indeed, other considerations make us think it opportune to repeat and to impress things which have been stated, but without sufficient emphasis.

The new school of economic thought, of which you are such a worthy representative, has a merit of no small significance. It has reacted against the anti-scientific tendencies of the historical and empirical schools, and has restored the concept of a science of *pure* economics. This means indeed nothing more than a science which is science ; the word pure, unless tautologous, is an explanation added for those who are ignorant or unmindful of what a science is. Economics is neither history nor discussion of practical issues : it is a science possessing its own principle, which is indeed called the *economic principle*.

But, as I had occasion to remark at another time,[1] I do not consider that this principle whose fundamental character is asserted, has hitherto been grasped in its individuality, nor conveniently defined in relation to other groups of facts, that is to the principles of other sciences. Of those conceptions of it which seem to me *erroneous*, the chief ones can be reduced to four which I will call the *mechanical*, the *hedonistic*, the *technological* and the *egoistic*.

You have now rejected the first two, because you think that mechanical and hedonistic consider-

[1] *Rivista di sociologia*, III. no. vi., pp. 746-8, see *Materialismio Storico*, pp. 193-208.

ations belong to metaphysics and psychology. But I acknowledge that I am dissatisfied with your method of arriving at this praiseworthy rejection.

You no longer say, indeed, as in your previous essay : ' L'économie pure n'est pas seulement semblable à la méchanique : c'est, à proprement parler, un genre de méchanique.' But you still say that ' Pure economics employs the same methods as rational mechanics, and has many points of contact with this science.' Although you do not pause over the mechanical considerations, it is not from a clear conviction that a datum in economics, as such, is quite different from a datum in mechanics ; but merely because it seems to you *convenient* to omit such considerations, of which you do not deny, but rather admit, the possibility.

Now I on the contrary, say decisively that the data of economics is not that of mechanics, or that there is no transition from the mechanical aspect of a fact to the economic aspect ; and that the very possibility of the mechanical point of view is excluded, not as a thing which may or may not be abstracted from, but as a contradiction in terms, which it is needful to shun.

Do you wish for the simplest and clearest proof of the non-mechanical nature of the economic principle ? Note, then, that in the data of economics a quality appears which is on the contrary repugnant to that of mechanics. *To an economic fact words can be applied which express approval or disapproval.* Man behaves economically *well* or *ill*, with *gain* or *loss*, *suitably* or *unsuitably* : he behaves, in short, *economically* or *uneconomically*. A fact in economics is, therefore, capable of *appraisement* (positive or negative) ; whilst a fact in mechanics is a mere fact, to which praise or blame can only be attached metaphorically.

It seems to me that on this point we ought easily to be agreed. To ascertain it, it is sufficient to appeal to internal observation. This shows us the fundamental distinction between the mechanical and the teleological, between mere fact and value. If I am not mistaken, you assign to metaphysics the problem of reducing the teleological to the mechanical, value to mere fact. But observe that metaphysics cannot get rid of the distinction ; and will only labour, with greater or less good luck, at its old business of *reconciling* opposites, or of *deriving two contraries from one unity.*

I foresee what may be advanced against this assertion of the non-mechanical nature of the economic principle. It may be said : What is not mechanical, is not measurable ; and economic values, on the contrary, *are measured.* Although hitherto the unit of measurement has not been found, it is yet a fact that we distinguish very readily *larger* and *smaller, greater* and least *values* and construct scales of values. This suffices to establish the *measurability* and hence the essentially mechanical nature of economic value. Look at the *economic man*, who has before him a series of possible actions a, b, c, d, e, f, . . . ; which have for him a decreasing value, indicated by the numbers 10, 9, 8, 7, 6 . . . just because he *measures* value, he decides on the action $a = 10$, and not on $c = 8$ or $f = 6$.

And there is no fault in the deduction granted the existence of the *scale of values*, which we have just illustrated by an example. *Granted the existence*: but, supposing this to be an *illusion* of ours? If the man in the example, instead of being the *homo œconomicus* were the *homo utopicus* or *heterocosmicus*, not to be found even in imaginative constructions?

This is precisely my opinion. The supposed *scale of values* is an absurdity. When the *homo œconomicus* in the given example, selects *a*, all the other actions (*b, c, d, e, f,* . . .) are not for him *values smaller than a* ; they are merely *non-a* ; they are what he rejects ; they are *non-values*.

If then the *homo œconomicus* could not have *a*, he would be acting *under different conditions* : under conditions without *a*. Change the conditions and the economic action—as is well known—changes also. And let us suppose that the conditions are such that, for the individual acting, *b* represents the action selected by him ; and *c, d, e, f,* . . . those which he omits to do, and which are all *non-b*, *i.e.* have no value.

If the conditions change again and it is supposed that the individual decides on *c*, and then on *d*, and then on *e*, and so on. These different economic actions, each *arising under particular conditions*, are *incommensurable* amongst themselves. They are *different* ; but each is perfectly adapted to the given conditions, and can only be judged *in reference to these conditions*.

But then what are these numbers, 10, 9, 8, 7, 6 . . . ? They are *symbols*, symbols of what ? What is the *reality* beneath the numerical symbol ? The reality is the *alteration in the actual conditions* ; and these numbers show a succession of changes: neither more nor less than is indicated by the alphabetic series, for which they are substituted.

The absurdity involved in the notion of greater or smaller values is, in short, the assumption that an individual may be *at the same moment* under different conditions. The *homo œconomicus* is not at the same moment in *a, b, c, d, e, f* . . . but when he is in *b*, he is no longer in *a* ; when he is in *c* he is no longer in *b*. He has before him only one action, approved by him ; this action rules out all the others which are infinite, and which for him are only *actions not preferred* (non-values).

Certainly physical objects form part of the data of economics ; and these, just because they are *physical*, are *measurable*. But economics does not consider physical things and objects, but *actions*. The physical object is merely the brute matter of an economic act : in measuring it we remain in the physical world, we do not pass over to that of economics, or else, when measured, the economic fact has become volatile. You say that ' political economy only concerns itself with choices, which fall on things that are variable in quantity and capable of measurement ' ; but pardon me, dear friend, you would be much perplexed if you had to justify this wholly arbitrary limitation ; and if you had to show that the attribute measurabilility influences in any way the attribute of belonging to economics.

I think that I have explained, shortly, but adequately for a wise man like yourself, the reasons why the mechanical conception of the economic principle is untenable. If calculations and measurements come into problems that are called economic they do so just in so far as these are not problems in *pure* economics.

This non-mechanical datum, which is an economic datum, you call *choice*. And this is all right. But *to choose* means to *choose consciously*. A choice made unconsciously, is either not a choice or not unconscious. You speak of the *unconscious actions* of man ; but these cannot be the *actions* of the man *in so far as he is man* but movements of man *in so far as he is also animal.* They are *instinctive* movements ; and instinct is not choice *except metaphorically.* Hence the examples you bring forward of dogs, of cats, of sparrows, of rats, and of asses from *Buridano,* are not facts of *choice* ; and hence are not economic facts. You consider animal economics as an unfruitful science, which exhausts itself in descriptions. Look more closely and you will see that this science does not exist. An economics of the animals, understood in the sense of the naturalists, has not been written, not because it is not worth while, but because *it is impossible to write it.* Whence could it be obtained unless from books such as the *Roman de Renart* and the *Animali parlanti* ?

This analysis ought to lead us to conceive of an economic datum as an act of man ; *i.e.* as a *fact of human activity*.

And from this recognition is inferred in its turn the true criticism of the *hedonistic* conception of the economic principle. You say that ' the equations of pure economics express merely the fact of a choice, and can be drawn up independently of the ideas of pleasure and pain,' but you admit at the same time that the fact of the *choice* ' can be expressed equally well as a fact of *pleasure*.'

It is true that every case of economic choice is at the same time, a case of *feeling* : of agreeable feeling if the economic choice is rightly made, of disagreeable feeling, if it is ill made. Man's activity develops itself in the human mind, not under a pneumatic bell, and an activity which develops rightly, brings as its reflex, a feeling of pleasure, that which develops badly, one of displeasure. What is economically useful, is, at the same time *pleasurable*.

But this judgment cannot be converted. The pleasurable is not always economically useful. The mistake in the hedonist theory consists in making this conversion. Pleasure may appear unaccompanied by man's activity, or may be accompanied by a human activity which is not economic. Herein lies the fundamental distinction between *pleasure* and *choice*. A choice, is in the concrete, inseparable from the feeling of pleasure and displeasure ; but this feeling is separable from *choice*, and may in fact exist independently of it.

If psychology be understood (as it is usually understood) as the science of psychical mechanism, economics is not a psychological science ; this Herr von Ehrenfels fails to grasp. I do not know whether you have read the two volumes hitherto published on the *System der Werttheorie*.[1] After devoting some hundred pages to psychological disquisitions—which I do not mean to discuss here—he wishes, finally, to prove that his definitions of value remain sound, from whatever theory of psychology you start. He does this as he asserts (§ 87), not because he is doubtful of himself, but to safeguard his economic conclusions, which are so important for the practical problems of life, from unjustified attacks based on the standpoints of schools of psychology other than his own, the method of the barrister, who composes an apparent conclusion, and makes several demands that are connected therewith *subordinately*. It is true that there is no need for economists to spend their time on details of theoretical psychology ; so true that Professor Ehrenfels might spare us his : but is it not true that economics remains the same *whatever psychological theory is accepted*. The unity of science

---

[1] DR CHRISTIAN V. EHRENFELS (Professor at Prague University) : *System der Werttheorie*, vol. I, *Allgemeine Werttheorie, Psychologie des Begehrens*, Leipzig, Reisland, 1897 ; vol. II, *Grundzüge einer Ethik*, the same, 1898.

means that a modification at one point is never without some reaction on the others ; and the reaction is greatest when it is a question of the way of conceiving two facts, distinct but inseparable, like the economic and the psychical fact.

An economic datum is not then a hedonistic datum, nor, in general, a mechanical datum. But as the fact of man's *activity*, it still remains to determine whether it is a fact of *knowledge* or of *will* : whether it is theoretical or practical.

You, who conceive it as choice, can have no doubt that it is a fact of practical activity, *i.e.* of *will*. This is also my own conclusion. *To choose* something can only mean *to will it*.

But you somewhat obscure the conclusion now indicated when you speak of *logical* and *illogical* actions, and place actions properly economic amongst the former. Logical and illogical bring us back to theoretical activity. A *logical* or *illogical* action is a common way of speaking ; but it is not a way of speaking exactly or accurately. The logical work of thought is quite distinct from the action of the will. To reason is not to will.

Nor is to will to reason ; but the will *presupposes* thought and hence logic. He who does not think, cannot even will. I mean by willing, what is known to us by the evidence of our consciousness ; not Schopenhauer's metaphysical *will*.

In *knowledge*, in so far as it is a necessary presupposition of economic action, is found, if not a justification, an explanation of your phrases about *logical and illogical actions.* Economic actions are always (we say so, at any rate) *logical* actions, *i.e.* preceded by logical acts. But it is necessary to distinguish carefully the two stages : the pheno-menon and its presupposition, since *from lack of distinction between the two stages has arisen the erroneous conception of the economic principle as a technological fact.* I have criticised at length in other essays this confusion between *technical* and *economic*, and I may be allowed to refer both to what I have written in my review of Stammler's book *Wirthschaft und Recht,* and to the more exact analyses in my recent memorandum on the *Estetica.* Stammler maintains precisely that the economic principle can be nothing but a technical concept. I would advise anyone who wishes to see at a glance, the difference between the technical and the economic to consider care-fully in what a *technical error* and in what an *economic error* respectively consist. A technical error is ignorance of the laws of the material on which we wish to work : for instance the belief that it is possible to put very heavy beams of iron on a delicate wall, without the latter falling into ruins. An *economic* error is the not aiming directly at one's own object ; to wish this and that, *i.e.* not really to wish either this or that. A technical error is an error of knowledge : an economic error is an error of will. He who makes a technical mistake will be called, if the mistake is a stupid one, an ignoramus ; he who makes an economic mistake, is a man who does not know how to behave in life : a weak and inconclusive person. And, as is well known and proverbial, people can be *learned* without being *men* (*practical* or *complete*).

Thus an economic fact is a fact of *practical activity*. Have we attained our object in this definition? Not yet. The definition is still incomplete and to complete it we must not only cross another expanse of sea, but avoid another rock : viz. that of the conception of economic data as *egoistic* data.

This error arises as follows : if an economic fact is a practical activity, it is still necessary to say how this activity is distinguished from moral activity. But moral activity is defined as *altruistic* ; then, it is inferred, economic data will be *egoistic*. Into this mistake has fallen, amongst others, our able Professor Pantaleoni, in his *Principî d'economia pura*, and in other writings.

The *egoistic* is not something merely *different* from a moral fact ; it is the *antithesis* of it ; it is the *immoral*. In this way, by making the economic principle equivalent to an egoistic fact, instead of distinguishing economics from morality, we should be subordinating the former to the latter, or rather should deny it any right to exist, recognising it as something merely negative, as a deviation from moral activity.

A datum in economics is quite different. It does not form an antithesis to a moral datum ; but is in the peaceable relation of condition to conditioned. It is the general condition which makes the rise of ethical activity possible. In the concrete, every action (volition) of man is either moral or

immoral, since no actions are *morally indifferent*.
But both the moral and the immoral are economic
actions; which means that the economic action,
taken by itself, is neither moral nor immoral.
Strength of character, for example, is needed both
by the honest man and by the cheat.

It seems to me that you approach gropingly to
this conception of the economic principle, as relating to practical actions, which taken in the
abstract, are neither moral nor immoral; when at
one point in your last essay, you exclude from
economic consideration *choices*, which have *an altruistic motive*; and further on, exclude also those
which are *immoral*. Now, since choices are necessarily
either altruistic or egoistic, either moral or immoral,
you have no way of escaping from the difficulty
except the one which I suggest; to regard economics
as concerned with practical activity in so far as it is
(abstractly) *emptied* of all *content, moral or immoral*.

I might enlarge further on this distinction and
show how it has an analogy in the sphere of theoretical activity, where the relation of economics to
ethics is repeated in the relation of æsthetics to
logic. And I might point out the reason why
scientific and æsthetic productions cannot be subjects of economic science, *i.e.* are not economic
products. The reason given, in this connection, by
Professor Ehrenfels, is, to say the least of it, curious:
he remarks that: 'the relations of value upon
which the data of logic and æsthetics rest, are so
simple that they do not demand a special economic

theory.' It should not be difficult to see that logical and æsthetic values are theoretical and not practical values, whereas economic value is a practical value, and that it is impossible to unite an *economics* of the *theoretical* as such. When, some years ago, the lamented Mazzola sent me the introduction in which he had discussed *Economics* and *Art*, I had occasion to write to him and afterwards to say to him by word of mouth, that much more fundamental relations might be discovered between the two groups of phenomena ; and he urged me to expound my observations and inquiries. This I have done in the essay on *Estetica*, referred to above. I am sorry to be obliged to *refer* so many times in writing to you and to the public. But here the need for brevity and clearness constrains me.

This, then, is a rapid statement of how I arrive at the definition of the data of economics, which I should like to see at the beginning of every economic treatise. *The data of economics are the practical activities of men in so far as they are considered as such, independent of any moral or immoral determination.*

Granted this definition, and it will be seen also that the concept of *utility*, or of *value* or of *ofelimity*, is nothing but the economic action itself, *in so far as it is rightly managed, i.e.* in so far as it is really economic. In the same way as *the true* is *thinking* activity itself, and *the good* is *moral* activity itself.

And to speak of things (physical objects) as having or not having value, will appear simply a metaphorical usage to express those *causes which we think efficacious to produce the effects* which we *desire*, and which are therefore our *ends*. *A* is worth *b*, the value of *a* is *b*, does not mean (the economists of the new school knew it well) $a=b$; nor even as is said $a > b$; but that *a* has *value* for us, and *b* has not. And value—as you know—exists only at *the moment of exchange, i.e. of choice.*

To connect with these general propositions the different problems which are said to belong to economic science, is the task of the writer of a special treatise on economics. It is your task, esteemed friend, if after having studied these general propositions, they seem to you acceptable. To me it seems that they alone are able to safeguard the independence of economics, not only as distinct from *History* and *Practice* but as distinct from *Mechanics, Psychology, Theory of Knowledge,* and *Ethics.*

Naples, 15th May 1900.[1]

II

Disagreement (1) *about method* (2) *postulates :* (1) *Nothing arbitrary in economic method, analogy of classificatory sciences erroneous :* (2) *Metaphysical postulate that facts of human activity same as physical facts erroneous : Definition of practical activity in so far as admits of definition : Moral and economic activity and approval : Economic and moral remorse ; Economic scale of values.*

Esteemed Friend,

Our disagreement concerning the nature of economic data has two chief sources :

[1] PARETO answered this letter in the same journal, *Giornale degli economisti,* August, 1900, pp. 139-162.

disagreement on a question of *method* and disagreement on a question of *postulates*. I acknowledge that one object of my first letter was to obtain from you such explanations as might set clearly in relief our disagreement on the two points indicated.— To reduce controversies to their simplest terms, to expose ultimate oppositions, is, you will agree, an approach to truth. I will explain briefly the two points at issue. In regard to that of method, although I agree with you in upholding the claims of a procedure that is logical, abstract and scientific, as compared with one that is historical (or synthetic, as you say), I cannot in addition allow that the former procedure involves something of the nature of an arbitrary choice, or that it can be worked out equally well in either of two ways. You talk of *cutting away* a *slice* from a concrete phenomenon, and examining this by itself; but I inquire how you manage to cut away that slice? for it is no question here of a piece of bread or of cheese into which we can actually put the knife, but of a series of representations which we have in our consciousness, and into which we can insert nothing except the light of our mental analysis. In order to cut off your slice you would thus have to carry out a logical analysis; *i.e.* to do at the outset what you propose to do subsequently. Your *cutting off of the slice* is indeed an answer to the problem of the *quid* in which an economic fact consists. You assume the existence of a test to distinguish what you take for the subject of your exposition from what you leave aside. But the test or guiding concept must be supplied by the very nature of the theory, and must be in conformity with it.

Would it for instance be in conformity with the nature of the thing, to cut away, as you wish to do, only that group of economic facts which relates to objects capable of measurement? What intrinsic connection is there between this merely accidental attribute, measurability, of the objects which enter into an economic action, and the economic action itself? Does measurability lead to a modification in the economic fact by changing its nature, *i.e.* by giving rise to *another* fact? If so, you must prove it. I, for my part, cannot see that an economic action changes its nature whether it relates to a sack of potatoes, or consists in an exchange of protestations of affection!

In your reply you refer to the need of avoiding waste of time over matters that are too simple, for which 'it is not worth while to set in motion the great machine of mathematical reasoning.' But this need relates to the pedagogy of the professional chair or of the book, not to the science in itself, which alone we are now discussing. It is quite evident that anybody who speaks or writes lays more stress on those portions which he thinks harder for his hearers and readers to grasp, or more useful to be told. But he who thinks, *i.e.* speaks with himself, pays attention to all portions without preferences and without omissions. We are now concerned with thought, that is with the *growth* of science ; not with the manner of *communicating* it. And in thought, we cannot admit arbitrary judgments.

Nor need we be turned aside by an analogy with the *classes* of facts, made by zoology and other natural sciences. The classifications of zoology and botany are not scientific operations, but merely views in perspective ; and, considered in relation to really scientific knowledge, they are arbitrary. He who investigates the nature of economic data, does not, however, aim at putting together, in perspective and roughly, groups of economic cases, as the zoologist or the botanist do, mutilating and manipulating the inexhaustible, infinite varieties of living creatures.

Upon the confusion between *a science* and the *exposition of a science* is based also the belief that we can follow different paths in order to arrive at a demonstration of the same truth. Unless in your case, since you are a mathematician, it arose from a false analogy with calculation. Now, calculation is not a science, because it does not give us the reasons of things ; and hence *mathematical* logic is logic in a manner of speaking, a variety of formal logic, and has nothing to do with *scientific* or inventive logic.

When we pass to the question of the postulates, you will certainly be surprised if I tell you that the disagreement between us consists in your wish to introduce a *metaphysical* postulate into economic science ; whereas I wish here to rule out every

metaphysical postulate and to confine myself entirely to the analysis of the given facts. The accusa-
tion of being *metaphysical* will seem to you the last
that could ever be brought against you. Your implied metaphysical postulate is, however, this ; that
the facts of man's activity are of the same nature
as physical facts ; that in the one case as in the
other we can only observe regularity and deduce
consequences therefrom, without ever penetrating
into the inner nature of the facts ; that these facts
are all alike *phenomena* (meaning that they would
presuppose a *noumena,* which evades us, and of
which they are manifestations). Hence whereas I
have called my essay ' On the economic *principle,*'
yours is entitled ' On the economic *phenomenon.*'

How could you defend this postulate of yours
except by a *metaphysical* monism ; for example that
of Spencer ? But, whilst Spencer was anti-meta-
physical and positivist in words, I claim the necessity of being so in deeds ; and hence I cannot
accept either *his* metaphysics or *his* monism, and I
hold to experience. This testifies to me the fundamental distinction between external and internal,
between physical and mental, between mechanics
and teleology, between passivity and activity, and
secondary distinctions involved in this fundamental
one. What metaphysics unites philosophy distinguishes (and joins together) ; the abstract contem-.
plation of unity is the death of philosophy. Let us
confine ourselves to the distinction between physical and mental. Whilst the external facts of nature,

admitted by empirical physical science, are always phenomena, since their source is by definition outside themselves, the internal facts or activities of man, cannot be called phenomena, since they are their own source.

By this appeal to experience and by this rejection of all metaphysical intrusion, I place myself in a position to meet the objection which you bring forward to my conception of economic data. You think that the ambiguity of the term *value* comes from this, that it denotes a very complex fact, a collection of facts included under a single word. For me, on the contrary, the difficulty in it arises from its denoting a very simple fact, a *summum genus*, *i.e.* the fact of the very *activity* of man. Activity is value. For us nothing is valuable except what is an effort of imagination, of thought, of will, of our activity in any of its forms. As Kant said that there was nothing in the universe that could be called *good* except the *good will*; so, if we generalise, it may be said that there is nothing in the universe that is valuable, except the *value of human activity*. Of value as of activity you cannot demand a so-called genetic definition. The simple and the original is genetically indefinable. Value is observed immediately in ourselves, in our consciousness.[1]

---

[1] I have before me Professor A. GRAZIADEI's article *Intorno alla teoria edonistica del valore*. (In *Riforma Sociale*, September 15th, 1900); in which A. fails to see how the purist theory of value dovetails in with the doctrines of Psychophysics and Psychology. I can well believe it! Psychophysics and Psychology are natural sciences and cannot throw light on economic fact

This observation shows us also that the *summum genus* 'value,' or 'mental activity' gives place to irreducible forms, which are in the first instance those of theoretical activity and practical activity, of theoretical values and practical values. But what does *practical* mean ?—you now ask me. I believe that I have already answered by explaining that the theoretical is everything which is a work of *contemplation*, and the practical everything that is the work of *will*. Is will an obscure term ? We may rather call the terms *light*, *warmth* and so on, obscure ; not that of *will*. What will is, I know well. I find myself face to face with it throughout my life as a man. Even in writing this letter, to-day, in a room in an inn, and in shaking off the laziness of country life, I have *willed* ; and if I have delayed the answer for two months, it is because I have been so feeble as not to know how to *will*.

You see from this that the question raised by me, whether by *choice* you meant *conscious* or *unconscious* choice, is not a *careless* question. It is equivalent to this other one ; whether the economic fact is or is not a fact of *will*. ' This does not alter

which is mental and of value. I may be allowed to point out, that, even three years ago, I gave a warning against the confusion of economics with psychology. (See in this volume pp. 72-75.) He who appeals to psychology (naturalistic) in order to understand economic fact, will always meet with the delusion, opportunely shown up by Graziadei. I have stated the reasons owing to which economics cannot dwell where the psychologists and hedonists say ; now Graziedei has questioned the door-keepers (Fechner, Wundt, etc.), and has learnt that it does not dwell there. Well and good !

the fact of the choice,' you say. But indeed it does alter it ! If we speak of *conscious* choice, we have before us a mental fact, if of *unconscious* choice, a natural fact ; and the laws of the former are not those of the latter. I welcome your discovery that economic fact is the fact of choice ; but I am *forced* to mean by *choice*, *voluntary* choice. Otherwise we should end by talking not only of the *choices* of a man who is *asleep* (when he moves from side to side) but of those of *animals*, and why not ? of *plants* and why not again ? of *minerals* ; passing rapidly along the steep slope down which my friend Professor C. Trivero has slipped in his recently published *Teoria dei bisogni*, for which may he be forgiven ! [1]

[1] CAMILLO TRIVERO, *La teoria dei bisogni*, Turin, Bocca, 1900, pp. 198. Trivero means by *need* ' the condition of a being, either conscious or unconscious (man, animal, plant, thing), in which it cannot remain ' : so that it can be said ' that all needs are ultimately condensed into the supreme *need* or *end* of being or becoming.' *Need* for him is hence actual reality itself. But since, on the other hand, he declares that he does not wish to solve nor even to consider the philosophical problem, it is hard to understand what a *theory of needs* (*i.e.* of reality) can be, and for what reason he goes back to such generalities.

It is true that Trivero believes that, by going back to the general concept of *need*, he can establish the *parent theory* on which rest the particular doctrines of needs ; and amongst them economics, which concerns itself with *economic* needs. If there are *species*—he says—we ought to determine of what *genus* they are species. But he will allow me to remark that the genus to look for is, as logic teaches, the *proximate* genus. To jump to such a great distance as to reality or to fact, would only lead to the noble discovery : that economic needs are part of reality, are a group of facts.

And what he does is to make an equally valuable discovery : that the true theory of history is the theory of needs, which,

When I defined economic data as 'the practical activities of man, in so far as they are considered as such, independently of any moral or immoral determination,' I did not make an arbitrary judgment, which might authorise others to do likewise, in a science which does not tolerate arbitrary judgments ; but I merely *distinguished* further within the species *practical activity*, two *sub-species* or grades : *pure* practical activity, (economic), and *moral* practical activity, (ethical) ; will that is merely economic, and moral will. There is ambiguity in your reproach that when I speak of approval or disapproval as aroused by economic activity, I am granted his definition of *needs*, is as much as to say that history is history of reality and the theory of it is—the theory.

I have then no objection to make to the meaning which Trivero wishes to give to the word *need* ; but I must assert that, having given it this meaning, he has not afterwards constructed the theory of anything, nor thrown light on any special group of facts.

For real economic theory his book is quite useless. Economists do not recognise the needs of things and plants and animals, but only human needs, or those of man in so far as he is *homo oeconomicus* and hence a conscious being. I too believe that it is right to work out philosophically the principle of economics ; but in order to do this, Trivero should have studied economic science. He declares that ' he does not want to hold fast to anyone's petticoats.' This statement is superfluous if it means that each individual ought to base his own scientific convictions on reason and not on authority. It is dangerous if it signifies, on the contrary, an intention to spare himself the trouble of studying other people's books, and of reconstructing everything from the beginning by his own personal efforts and by the aid of general culture alone. The result obtained—being far from satisfactory—should deter the author (who will not grumble at my plain speaking), from returning to this unfruitful method in the future.

considering the matter from a *synthetic* instead of an analytic point of view, and that approval or disapproval are *extraneous* factors. I did not however speak (and I believed that I had explained myself clearly), of *moral, intellectual* or *æsthetic* approval or disapproval. No, I said, and I repeat, that a judgment of approval or reprobation was necessarily bound up with economic activity : but a *merely* ECONOMIC judgment of approval or reprobation. ' *By saying* that Rhenish wine is *useful* to me, has a *value* for me, is *ofelimo* to me, I mean only to say that I like it ; and I do not see how this simplest of relations can be well or ill-managed.' You will forgive me if in this sentence of yours I have italicised the words *by saying*. Here is the point. Certainly the mere *saying* does not give rise to an internal judgment of economic approval or disapproval. It will give rise to a grammatical or linguistic, *i.e.* æsthetic, approval or disapproval, according to whether the saying is clear or confused, well or ill expressed. But it is no question of *saying* : it is a question of *doing*, *i.e.* of the action willed carried out by the movement that is willed, of a *choice* of movement. And do you think that the acquisition and consumption of a bottle of Rhenish wine involves no judgment of approval or disapproval ? If I am very rich, if my aim in life is to obtain momentary sensual pleasures, and I know that Rhenish wine will secure me one of them, I buy and drink Rhenish wine and approve my act. I am satisfied with myself. But if I do not *wish* to indulge in gluttony, and if my money is all devoted to other purposes, for which I *wish* as preferable, and if, in spite of this, yielding to the temptation of the moment, I buy and drink Rhenish wine, I have put myself into contradiction with myself, and the sensual pleasure will be followed by a judgment of disapproval, by a legitimate and fitting ECONOMIC REMORSE.

To prove to you how, in all this, I omit every *moral* consideration, I will give you another example : that of a knave who thinks it *ofelimo* to himself to murder a man in order to rob him of a sum of money. At the moment of assassination, and although remaining a knave at heart, he yields to an emotion of fear or to a pathological feeling of compassion, and does not kill the man. Note carefully the terms of the hypothesis. The knave will call himself an ass and an imbecile, and will feel *remorse* for his contradictory and inconclusive conduct ; but not indeed a *moral* remorse (of that he is, by hypothesis, incapable), but, precisely, a remorse that is merely *economic*.

It seems to me that there is another confusion, easy to dispel, in your counter criticism to my criticism of the *scale of values* (economic) you say that 'there is no need for one person to find himself at the same moment under different conditions ; it is enough that he can *picture to himself* these different conditions.' Can you in truth *picture yourself* being *at the same moment* under *different* conditions ? Fancy has its laws ; and does not allow the imagination of what is unimaginable. You can easily *say* that you *picture* it to yourself : words are docile ; but, to picture it *in reality*, is, pardon me, another matter altogether. You will not succeed in it any more than I. Ask me to imagine a lion with the head of a donkey, and I will comply at once ; but ask me to imagine a lion standing *at the same moment* in two different places, and I cannot succeed. I will picture to myself, if you like, two similar lions, two exactly alike, but not the same in two different positions. Fancy reconstructs reality, but possible reality, not the impossible or what is contradictory. Thus my demonstration of the absurdity of the *scale of values* applies both to actual and to possible reality. Nay, in discussing science in the abstract it was framed precisely on the mere consideration of the possible.

I do not know whether I have answered all your objections, but I have endeavoured to answer all those which seem to me fundamental. A dispute, in which questions of method and of principle are at stake need not be carried on pedantically into minute details ; we must depend to some extent on the assistance of the readers, who, putting themselves mentally in the position of the two disputants, work out for themselves the final application. I wish merely to add that it is my strongest conviction that the reaction against metaphysics (a far-sighted reaction in that it has freed scientific procedure from admixture with the arbitrary judgments of feeling and belief) has been pushed forward by

many so far as to destroy science itself. The mathe
maticians who have a quick feeling for scientific
procedure, have done much for economic science
by reviving in it the dignity of abstract analysis,
darkened and overwhelmed by the mass of anec-
dotes of the historical school. But, as it happens,
they have also introduced into it the prejudice of
their profession, and, being themselves students
of the general conditions of the physical world, the
particular prejudice that mathematics can take up
in relation to economics—which is the science of
man, of a form of the conscious activity of man—
the same attitude which it rightly takes up in relation to the empirical natural sciences.

From what I have now stated you will easily
discover exactly how far we are in agreement in
the establishment of the principles of *Economics*
and how far we disagree. If my new observations
should assist in further reducing the extent of the
disagreement, I shall indeed be glad.

Perugia, 20*th October*, 1900.[1]

---

[1] PARETO answers this second letter in the *Giornale degli economisti*, February, 1901, pp. 131-138.

INDEX OF NAMES *

* Marx's name is omitted.   The Asterisks indicate notes.